Family Favorite
Casserole Recipes

Family Favorite Casserole Recipes

103 Comforting Breakfast Casseroles,
Dinner Ideas, and Desserts
Everyone Will Love

Addie Gundry

St. Martin's Griffin ⚘ New York

Photography by Tom Krawczyk

www.stmartins.com

The Library of Congress Cataloging-in-Publication Data is available upon request.

ISBN 978-1-250-12334-3 (trade paperback)
ISBN 978-1-250-12335-0 (e-book)

Our books may be purchased in bulk for promotional, educational, or business use. Please contact your local bookseller or the Macmillan Corporate and Premium Sales Department at 1-800-221-7945, extension 5442, or by e-mail at MacmillanSpecialMarkets@macmillan.com.

First Edition: June 2017

10 9 8 7 6 5 4 3 2 1

To ACG, *my favorite taste tester.*
Thank you for always being hungry; for eating
the good and the bad, the sweet and the spicy; and for
turning a blind eye when things burn.

Contents

4
Beef and Pork

5
Vegetarian

6
Healthy

7
Internationally Inspired

8
Dessert

Introduction

A casserole is something to be shared—something warm, rich, usually ooey-gooey, and worthy of a gathering on its own. I imagine something cheesy, like Smoked Gouda Mac and Cheese (page 39), at the center of a table, bright-patterned linens, flowers, maybe bread crumbs or a fading stain from spilled wine. I picture laughing parents talking about their day, a sticky little hand reaching in for dessert, and full plates leaving saucy stains behind.

I was born and raised not far from my grandparents' farm in Minnesota. I spent most of my childhood there, and after growing up on cheesy corn-filled home-style meals, I flew far overseas to be classically trained in French cuisine. I went from mashing potatoes in a country kitchen to precisely dicing them in a three-Michelin-starred restaurant in Avignon, France, and it is safe to say that my days of making casseroles came to a screeching halt. I spent the next several years in fine dining entertaining and innovation, only to end up right back in the Midwest, making casseroles in my home kitchen. The reason is simple—I realized that I was passionate about combining ease with elegance. A dish doesn't have to be complicated to be creative. You don't need multiple pots and pans to find flavor. And with the proper tools, tips, and techniques, anyone can cook memorable meals. The beauty behind these dishes is their simplicity, but each is packed with flavor and worthy of a photo, characteristics that give you reason to whip up these family favorites any day of the week.

One of my favorites is the Country Chicken and Spinach Casserole (page 67). The Party Popper Potato Puff Casserole (page 36) is the perfect thing to bring to a soccer game or a tailgate, and will be welcomed with open arms on a cold autumn day. The Layered Ham and Cheese Croissant Casserole (page 4) is my go-to brunch recipe, and the 20-Minute Chocolate Candy Cookie Casserole (page 212) is a quick and easy crowd-pleasing dessert! You'll find my recipe for Easy Baked Goulash (page 197), a beef casserole that I made while filming on the Food Network; and One-Pot Chicken Cordon Bleu Casserole (page 79), a dish that reminds me of when my husband and I first started dating.

I've used my experience and excitement for food and entertaining to create each one of these 103 casseroles in a unique way. Why 103? When you come to my house for dinner, I want you to know you can always bring a friend, or two, or three . . . and for those who have been to my home, you know firsthand that guests tend to multiply as the food continues to come out of the oven and cocktails are poured. One hundred recipes felt too rigid, too finite. By adding the extra three it became more welcoming, a reminder that there is always more room at the table, especially when a casserole sits in the center of it.

1

Breakfast

From steel-cut oats packed with berries to light and

fluffy cinnamon-coated rolls, fried eggs over hash browns,

and spicy charred sausage with avocado, breakfast

casseroles come in all shapes and sizes.

Layered Ham and Cheese Croissant Casserole

Yield: 7 large croissant sandwiches | Prep Time: 20 minutes plus overnight set | Cook Time: 1 hour

Nothing says brunch, and morning comfort, like a ham and cheese croissant. This casserole can be made the night before, which makes things even easier in the morning. Serve straight out of the casserole dish as individual sandwiches, or cut up and place on a platter. I like to shingle the croissants so they're easy to grab out of the dish individually. Either way, find yourself some flaky croissants and kick off your weekend!

INGREDIENTS

7 croissants

2 tablespoons Dijon mustard

14 thin slices deli ham

7 slices Swiss cheese

10 large eggs

1½ cups whole milk

½ teaspoon salt

½ teaspoon freshly ground black pepper

DIRECTIONS

1. Lightly coat a 9 × 13-inch baking dish with cooking spray.

2. Slice the croissants, spread each one with mustard, and fill them with the ham and cheese. Shingle the croissant sandwiches into the casserole dish.

3. Beat the eggs in a medium bowl, add the milk, salt, and pepper, and mix well. Pour over the sandwiches and cover the dish with foil. Weight the top with a plate or cookie sheet to submerge the sandwiches in the egg mixture and refrigerate for at least 4 hours or overnight.

4. Preheat the oven to 350°F. Bake, covered with the foil, for 30 minutes. Remove the foil and bake for an additional 30 minutes. Serve.

VARIATIONS

Spice the sandwiches up with pepper jack cheese or add a touch of sweetness with honey Dijon mustard.

NOTES

It's all about the croissants! If you can find some at a local bakery, the superior quality and freshness will certainly shine through.

Berry Breakfast Casserole

Yield: Serves 6 | Prep Time: 20 minutes | Cook Time: 40 minutes

This casserole looks and tastes like a blondie, but it's packed with oats and superfood berries. Prepare it in the morning before guests arrive. If you have a few stragglers, pop the casserole back in the oven to reheat when everyone is ready to eat. If there is any left after breakfast, this makes for one of my favorite afternoon snacks served with yogurt and honey.

INGREDIENTS

1 cup old-fashioned rolled oats

1 cup steel-cut oats

1 cup all-purpose flour

1 cup light brown sugar

1 teaspoon baking powder

½ teaspoon salt

1 large egg

1 cup whole milk

¼ cup vegetable oil

1 teaspoon vanilla extract

1 cup blueberries

1 cup raspberries

½ cup dried cranberries

½ cup coarsely chopped pecans

1 cup strawberries, hulled and quartered

Yogurt and honey, for serving

DIRECTIONS

1. Preheat the oven to 350°F and lightly coat an 8 × 8-inch baking dish with cooking spray.

2. In a large bowl, combine the oats, flour, brown sugar, baking powder, and salt.

3. Beat the egg in a small bowl, add the milk, oil, and vanilla, and mix well. Stir the wet ingredients into the dry, add the blueberries, raspberries, cranberries, and pecans, and mix until well blended.

4. Pour into the baking dish and bake for 40 minutes. Remove from the oven and top with the sliced strawberries. Cut into squares and serve warm with yogurt and honey.

Make-Ahead Oatmeal Casserole

Yield: Serves 6 | Prep Time: 15 minutes | Cook Time: 30 minutes

Before you crawl under the covers at night, assemble this oatmeal and set it in the fridge. When you wake up, all you have to do is brew a pot of coffee and pop the dish in the oven. The sweet blueberries folded throughout and the taste of buttery vanilla almonds make this a very special oatmeal. This casserole tastes like comfort and warmth on a cold winter weekend.

INGREDIENTS

2 cups rolled oats

⅓ cup plus 2 tablespoons light brown sugar

1 teaspoon baking powder

1 teaspoon ground cinnamon

½ teaspoon kosher salt

½ cup dried cherries

½ cup blueberries, plus extra for serving

¼ cup toasted almonds

1 cup whole milk

1 cup half-and-half

1 large egg

2 tablespoons unsalted butter, melted and cooled

1 teaspoon vanilla bean paste or vanilla extract

Honey and yogurt, for serving

DIRECTIONS

1. Preheat the oven to 375°F and lightly coat an 8 × 8-inch baking dish with cooking spray.

2. In a large bowl, combine the oats, ⅓ cup of the brown sugar, the baking powder, cinnamon, salt, dried cherries, half of the blueberries, and half of the almonds. Pour into the baking dish and top with the remaining blueberries and almonds. Whisk together the milk, half-and-half, egg, melted butter, and vanilla and pour on top of the oatmeal mixture.

3. At this point you can either sprinkle with the remaining 2 tablespoons brown sugar and bake for 30 minutes, or cover as is and place in the fridge overnight.

4. Once baked, remove from oven and scoop into individual serving bowls. Serve warm, topped with extra blueberries, yogurt, and honey if you wish.

Cinnamon Roll Casserole

Yield: Serves 8 | Prep Time: 15 minutes | Cook Time: 30 minutes

We all know the smell of cinnamon rolls baking, the stickiness that comes with eating a vanilla-glazed sweet bun, and the burst of powdered sugar glaze and warm raisins when we take the first bite. But I'll bet that most often you bake cinnamon rolls in a single layer on a cookie sheet in the oven. I guarantee this version, layered in a casserole dish and dredged in cinnamon sugar batter, will be the ooey-gooiest in your recipe collection.

INGREDIENTS

Casserole

2 (12-ounce) tubes cinnamon rolls

¼ cup light brown sugar

1½ cups raisins

4 large eggs

½ cup heavy cream

2 tablespoons maple syrup

2 teaspoons vanilla extract

1 teaspoon ground cinnamon

¼ teaspoon ground nutmeg

Cream Cheese Icing

4 ounces cream cheese, room temperature

1 cup powdered sugar

4 tablespoons unsalted butter, room temperature

½ teaspoon vanilla extract

DIRECTIONS

1. Preheat the oven to 350°F and lightly coat a 9-inch pie plate with cooking spray.

2. Arrange a layer of the cinnamon rolls to completely cover the bottom of the pie plate. Sprinkle 2 tablespoons of the brown sugar, then ½ cup raisins, over the cinnamon rolls. Whisk together the eggs, cream, maple syrup, vanilla, cinnamon, and nutmeg and pour over the rolls. Place the remaining rolls on top and sprinkle with the remaining brown sugar and ½ cup raisins. Bake for 30 minutes, until the top is golden brown.

3. For the cream cheese icing: While the cinnamon rolls are baking, prepare the icing by combining the cream cheese, powdered sugar, butter, and vanilla with a whisk or hand mixer until smooth.

4. Drizzle the cream cheese icing over the hot cinnamon rolls and top with the remaining raisins. Serve.

Chocolate Chip Buttermilk Pancake Casserole

Yield: Serves 4 | Prep Time: 20 minutes plus 2 hours' refrigeration | Cook Time: 40 minutes

On Saturdays I make pancakes. Not because they are complicated or because I never seem to have time during the week, but because they are decadent and worthy of a weekend occasion. I am not sure when this tradition started, but it began with standard pancake making and one day a week I would work on pouring perfect pancakes, which never seemed to look too circular. My solution? Turn them into a casserole! Not only is it easier, but it happens to be delicious, while delivering that spot-hitting Saturday pancake essence.

INGREDIENTS

4 large eggs

1 cup heavy cream

¼ cup maple syrup

1 teaspoon vanilla bean paste or vanilla extract

40 mini buttermilk pancakes, homemade or store-bought, frozen and thawed

2 bananas, thinly sliced

½ cup mini semisweet chocolate chips

¼ cup bittersweet chocolate chips

Powdered sugar

DIRECTIONS

1. Lightly coat an 8-inch round cake pan with cooking spray. Whisk together the eggs, cream, maple syrup, and vanilla.

2. Layer half of the pancakes in the pan and scatter 1 sliced banana and half of the chocolate chips on top. Pour half of the egg mixture over the pancakes. Repeat with the remaining pancakes, banana, chocolate chips, and egg mixture. Cover the dish with plastic wrap and refrigerate for 2 hours.

3. Half an hour before you're ready to bake the casserole, preheat the oven to 350°F. Remove the plastic wrap and cover the dish with foil. Bake the casserole, covered, for 30 minutes, then remove the foil and bake for an additional 10 minutes. Dust with powdered sugar and serve.

VARIATIONS

If you prefer a basic buttermilk pancake casserole, remove the chocolate chips. I love how mini pancakes look; I think they are adorable! But of course you can use full-size pancakes and cut them in quarters before placing them in the baking dish.

Cinnamon-Pumpkin French Toast

Yield: Serves 6 to 8 | Prep Time: 20 minutes | Cook Time: 45 minutes

I have a vivid memory of carving pumpkins with a friend on a cold fall weekend in New England. We wore cozy sweaters, drank tea, and spent the majority of the day on the floor scooping and sifting the pumpkin seeds out while a dog lapped around, doing her best to lick them up. There are plenty of things to make with pumpkin, namely that ubiquitous pie, but this is by far one of my favorite pumpkin recipes. The challah bread is sliced thick, resembling the French toast sticks I ate as a kid, and coated in a sweet cinnamon-pumpkin mixture.

INGREDIENTS

French Toast

2 teaspoons unsalted butter

1 cup heavy cream

3 large eggs

¼ cup sugar

1 tablespoon ground cinnamon

1 teaspoon vanilla extract

¼ teaspoon ground ginger

¼ teaspoon ground nutmeg

¼ teaspoon kosher salt

1 (8-ounce) can pumpkin puree

1 large loaf brioche or challah bread, sliced into 2-inch sticks

Streusel Topping

1 cup light brown sugar

¾ cup pecans, roughly chopped

4 tablespoons unsalted butter, cold, cut into ¼-inch cubes

2 teaspoons ground cinnamon

Maple Butter

8 tablespoons unsalted butter, melted

2 tablespoons pure maple syrup

DIRECTIONS

1. Preheat the oven to 350°F and butter a 9 × 13-inch baking dish.

2. For the French toast: Combine the cream, eggs, sugar, cinnamon, vanilla, ginger, nutmeg, and salt in a large bowl. Whisk in the pumpkin puree until smooth. Place the bread sticks in the baking dish, add the pumpkin mixture, and gently toss to coat.

3. For the streusel topping: Gently combine the brown sugar, pecans, butter, and cinnamon in a small bowl.

4. Sprinkle the streusel topping over the casserole and bake for 40 to 45 minutes, until set (if the streusel starts to brown, cover with foil to finish baking).

5. For the maple butter: While the casserole bakes, combine the melted butter with maple syrup in a small bowl.

6. Scoop the French toast into serving bowls and serve drizzled with maple butter.

Overnight Eggs Benedict

Yield: Serves 6 to 8 | Prep Time: 20 minutes plus overnight set | Cook Time: 1 hour

I thought eggs Benedict was a restaurant-only food, too challenging to replicate at home. But my, was I wrong! And the real kicker? This version is made the night before, so you don't have to do any work in the morning. With sliced ham and English muffins baked in eggs and topped with a simple hollandaise, this may not look like the eggs Benedict you're familiar with, but its taste rivals some of the best.

INGREDIENTS

6 large eggs

1 cup half-and-half

3 scallions, chopped

1 teaspoon salt

2 (7-ounce) ham steaks, cut into ½-inch dice

6 English muffins, toasted and cut into 1-inch cubes

½ teaspoon paprika

1 cup whole milk

1 (.9-ounce) package hollandaise sauce mix

4 tablespoons unsalted butter

Fresh parsley, for garnish

DIRECTIONS

1. Lightly coat a 9 × 13-inch baking dish with cooking spray. Whisk together the eggs, half-and-half, scallions, and salt.

2. Spread half of the ham in the baking dish. Place the toasted English muffin cubes on top of the ham and then top with the remaining ham. Pour the egg mixture over the casserole, cover, and refrigerate overnight.

3. Heat the oven to 375°F. Sprinkle the paprika over the casserole, cover with foil, and bake for 45 minutes. Remove the foil and bake until the egg mixture is set, an additional 15 minutes.

4. Meanwhile, whisk the milk and hollandaise sauce mix together in a saucepan. Add the butter and bring to a boil, stirring. Lower the heat to a simmer and stir until thick. Drizzle the sauce over the casserole and serve, garnished with parsley sprigs.

VARIATIONS

Use whole-wheat English muffins for a healthier alternative.

Bacon and Egg Hash Brown Scramble

Yield: Serves 8 | Prep Time: 15 minutes | Cook Time: 1 hour

"Scramble" is one of my favorite words. You might think chaos and mass confusion, but when it comes to a baked breakfast, that word works well. Inside this mixture are hash browns, bacon, cheddar, and eggs—and when those come together, no order is the order of the day.

INGREDIENTS

2 large eggs

1 (10.75-ounce) can cheddar cheese soup

1 cup evaporated milk

1 tablespoon chopped fresh thyme

¼ teaspoon salt

¼ teaspoon freshly ground black pepper

1 (20-ounce) bag frozen hash browns, thawed

6 strips bacon, cooked and chopped

1 cup shredded cheddar cheese

1 cup corn flakes, crushed

2 tablespoons unsalted butter, melted

DIRECTIONS

1. Preheat the oven to 350°F and lightly coat an 8 × 8-inch baking dish with cooking spray.

2. In a large bowl, beat the eggs until frothy. Add the soup, milk, thyme, salt, and pepper and whisk to mix well. Stir in the hash browns and bacon until well mixed. Pour into the baking dish and top with the cheese. Place the crushed corn flakes in the bowl, add the melted butter, and toss to coat; sprinkle evenly on top of the casserole.

3. Bake for 1 hour, until puffy and lightly browned on top. Serve.

NOTES

Evaporated milk will give the mixture a creamier texture, but can be replaced with whole or 2 percent milk.

Chicken Ranch Hash Brown Casserole

Yield: Serves 2 | Prep Time: 15 minutes | Cook Time: 30 minutes

The first moment when your fork punctures the yolk is the start of a delicious meal as the ooey-gooeyness coats the rest of the dish, acting as a last-minute sauce. Crispy ranch hash browns and chicken make for a hearty breakfast, one that happens to be a perfect dish for two.

INGREDIENTS

1 cup canned cream of chicken soup

3 tablespoons sour cream

2 ounces cream cheese, room temperature

2 tablespoons whole milk

1 tablespoon ranch dressing and seasoning mix

3 drops Tabasco, plus extra for serving

Salt and freshly ground black pepper

2 cups frozen hash browns with bell pepper and onion, thawed

1 boneless, skinless chicken breast, cooked and shredded, approximately 1 cup when shredded

½ cup shredded cheddar cheese

2 teaspoons unsalted butter, melted

2 large eggs

Fresh parsley, for garnish (optional)

DIRECTIONS

1. Preheat the oven to 350°F and lightly coat an 8 × 8-inch baking dish with cooking spray.

2. In a medium bowl combine the soup, sour cream, cream cheese, milk, ranch mix, Tabasco, and ¼ teaspoon pepper. Stir to mix, then add the hash browns, chicken, and cheese. Spoon into the baking dish and bake for 30 minutes, until the mixture is bubbling and the top is lightly browned.

3. In a small skillet, melt the butter over medium heat, then crack the eggs into the pan and season with salt and pepper. After 3 minutes, when the eggs begin to whiten, flip them. Divide the casserole between two plates, top each portion with a fried egg, and serve, garnished with fresh parsley if desired.

NOTES

For the chicken, use leftovers from dinner or a rotisserie chicken from the store.

Southwest Breakfast Bake

Yield: Serves 6 to 8 | Prep Time: 20 minutes | Cook Time: 55 minutes

My husband and I got married in the hot desert of Arizona. Traditionally, a breakfasting bride eats tea sandwiches and a few grapes and does a quick toast with a light, bubbly champagne. But I took a different approach. Embracing the bright colors and flavors of the Southwest, this breakfast bake is a jumble of ingredients that perfectly combine for a zesty morning start.

INGREDIENTS

1 pound bulk pork sausage

1½ cups diced red bell pepper

1 cup chopped onion

1 (15-ounce) can chili with beans

½ teaspoon salt

1 (11-ounce) can tomatillos, well drained

1 (4.5-ounce) can mild green chiles, well drained

½ cup sour cream

6 large eggs

½ cup whole milk

1 cup shredded cheddar cheese

3 cups frozen plain hash browns, thawed

1 teaspoon chili powder

1 teaspoon ground cumin

1 avocado, diced

Tortillas, salsa, sour cream, and cilantro for serving

DIRECTIONS

1. Preheat the oven to 375°F and lightly coat a 9 × 13-inch baking dish with cooking spray.

2. In a large skillet, brown the sausage over medium-high heat for about 8 minutes, stirring frequently, until the edges of the meat are brown. Add the bell pepper and onion and cook for an additional 3 minutes. (The meat does not need to be fully cooked; it will finish in the oven.) Add the chili to the meat mixture and stir to combine.

3. Place the salt, tomatillos, chiles, and sour cream in a blender or food processor and blend well. Add the eggs and milk and blend. Add half the cheese and blend briefly.

4. Spread the meat mixture in the baking dish, then add the hash browns. Sprinkle with the chili powder and cumin. Pour the sour cream mixture on top and sprinkle with the remaining cheese. Bake for 45 minutes, until the mixture is set and the top is bubbly and browned. Serve with avocado, tortillas, salsa, sour cream, and cilantro.

Loaded Omelet Casserole

Yield: Serves 6 | Prep Time: 20 minutes | Cook Time: 45 minutes

When I told my family that I was going to culinary school instead of a traditional college, they thought I was crazy. They wondered who would want to spend Saturday mornings in a kitchen flipping eggs. I have since graduated to a larger career in the culinary world, but cooking eggs is and always will be a big part of that. After many years of egg cookery, what I have realized is that you don't always need to make a fancy egg dish when you can make an omelet casserole, especially on a relaxing Saturday in pajamas. Throw your favorite ingredients into one bowl and pour them into a pie plate to bake. I like mine with lean ground turkey and kale for extra protein, but you can make it any way you choose. This loaded omelet casserole is easy to customize.

INGREDIENTS

1 onion, diced

1 red bell pepper, diced

2 tablespoons olive oil

1 pound ground turkey

1 cup kale, chopped

8 large eggs

1 cup whole milk

1 cup shredded Gruyère cheese

1 teaspoon salt

1 teaspoon freshly ground black pepper

½ teaspoon crushed red pepper flakes

DIRECTIONS

1. Preheat the oven to 375°F and lightly coat a 9-inch pie plate with cooking spray.

2. In a large skillet, sauté the onion and red bell pepper in olive oil over medium heat for 3 minutes. Add the ground turkey and cook until browned, 7 to 8 minutes. Add the kale and sauté for 2 minutes, until slightly wilted.

3. Beat the eggs and milk in a large mixing bowl. Add the cooked turkey mixture, cheese, salt, black pepper, and red pepper flakes to the egg mixture. Pour the egg mixture into the pie plate and bake uncovered for 30 minutes, or until the eggs are set. Cut into wedges and serve.

VARIATIONS

Love mushrooms? Add those, too! This is your catch-all loaded egg casserole, so experiment with vegetables. The more the merrier. Vegetarian? Omit the ground turkey.

Bacon Potato Quiche Casserole

Yield: Serves 6 | Prep Time: 45 minutes | Cook Time: 1 hour

When I think of quiche, I think light and airy, served with a glass of champagne at a ladies' lunch. Well, this is not that kind of dainty quiche. If you like the consistency and flavor profile of a quiche but are hoping for a heartier dish, then you are in luck. Within the rich egg custard, crisp roasted potatoes and salty bacon add a welcome texture and crunch.

INGREDIENTS

4 to 6 russet potatoes, peeled and cut into 2-inch cubes

¼ cup olive oil

Salt and freshly ground black pepper

2 tablespoons unsalted butter

1 onion, diced

2 garlic cloves, minced

8 large eggs

⅓ cup whole milk

1 pound bacon, cooked and chopped

1 cup shredded cheddar cheese

1 teaspoon cayenne pepper

Thyme

DIRECTIONS

1. Preheat the oven to 400°F and lightly coat a 9 × 13-inch baking dish with cooking spray.

2. Toss the potatoes with the olive oil, ½ teaspoon salt, and ½ teaspoon pepper to coat, then place on a baking sheet. Roast for 30 minutes, until lightly browned. Remove the potatoes and lower the oven temperature to 350°F.

3. In a medium skillet, melt the butter over medium heat, then add the onion and garlic and cook until softened.

4. In a large bowl, beat the eggs and milk. Add the cooked potatoes, sautéed onion, bacon, cheese, and cayenne and season with salt and pepper.

5. Pour into the baking dish and bake for 25 minutes, until the egg custard is set. Sprinkle with thyme and serve.

Grandma's Biscuits and Gravy Casserole

Yield: Serves 6 to 8 | Prep Time: 20 minutes | Cook Time: 45 minutes

My grandmother raised four children on a farm in the middle of nowhere (sorry, Grandma, but it's true), Minnesota. If anyone were to make biscuits and gravy on a regular basis, you better believe it was Leatrice! I can't count how many times I helped out in that tiny kitchen, but the smell is something I certainly remember. You too may have a memory that includes biscuits and gravy. It may not be from a cliché farmhouse with a tractor in the background, but whether from a drive-through, that time you went to Texas, or a weekend camping, I would bet the dish was comforting. Flaky, buttery biscuits drenched in creamy sauce and served with sausage, this recipe nourishes your belly and soul.

INGREDIENTS

1 (16.3-ounce) can flaky biscuits

8 ounces turkey breakfast sausage

2 tablespoons unsalted butter

¼ cup all-purpose flour

3 cups whole milk

½ teaspoon salt

½ teaspoon freshly ground black pepper

¼ teaspoon cayenne pepper

DIRECTIONS

1. Preheat the oven to 400°F and lightly coat a 7 × 11-inch baking dish with cooking spray.

2. Cut the biscuits into quarters and place half of the biscuits in the baking dish. Bake for 10 minutes.

3. While the biscuits are baking, brown the sausage in a skillet over medium heat until fully cooked. Remove and drain. Add the butter to the empty skillet and melt over low heat. Then whisk in the flour and cook for 2 minutes. Add the milk, salt, pepper, and cayenne, bring to a low boil, and cook until thick. Return the sausage to the skillet with the gravy and stir to combine.

4. Pour the mixture over the biscuits and layer the remaining biscuits on top. Bake for 30 minutes, until the top of the casserole is golden brown. Serve.

Sausage Fajita Frittata

Yield: Serves 6 to 8 | Prep Time: 25 minutes | Cook Time: 1 hour

During a weekend in California where my husband and I (and a whole bunch of friends) attended a day time country music festival, this spicy fajita frittata became the most desired dish, set out on the pool patio table with salsa and chips, a bowl of guacamole, and cold beers. It's the perfect thing to wake up to, graze through, and serve for breakfast, brunch, or lunch.

INGREDIENTS

3 cups Southern-style frozen hash browns

2 teaspoons olive oil

1 red bell pepper, cut into strips

1 green bell pepper, cut into strips

1 small poblano pepper, cut into strips

12 ounces turkey breakfast sausage

1 red onion, cut into strips

1 garlic clove, minced

6 large eggs

⅓ cup half-and-half

1 teaspoon dried oregano

1 teaspoon kosher salt

½ teaspoon freshly ground black pepper

1½ cups shredded Mexican cheese blend

DIRECTIONS

1. Preheat the oven to 450°F and lightly coat a 9 × 13-inch baking dish with cooking spray.

2. Pour the hash browns over the bottom of the baking dish and bake for 20 minutes.

3. Meanwhile, in a large skillet, heat the olive oil over medium heat. Add the bell peppers and poblano pepper and cook for 5 minutes. Add the sausage, onion, and garlic and cook until the sausage is fully cooked.

4. Remove the hash browns from the oven and lower the oven temperature to 350°F. Top the hash browns with the sausage mixture. Whisk the eggs, half-and-half, oregano, salt, and pepper in a bowl until combined and pour over the casserole. Sprinkle the cheese on top and bake for 25 minutes, until the eggs are set. Serve.

Ham and Biscuit Breakfast Casserole

Yield: Serves 6 to 8 | Prep Time: 30 minutes | Cook Time: 20 minutes

This screams "Sunday supper." After a relaxing day of laundry, football, and backyard chores, this creamy ham casserole, partnered with homemade biscuits, is one of my favorite ways to end a great weekend, and an even better way to start a good week.

INGREDIENTS

1 tablespoon vegetable oil

1 (8-ounce) ham steak, cut into ½-inch dice

⅓ cup chopped onion

¼ cup chopped green bell pepper

2¼ cups plus 1 tablespoon all-purpose flour

1 (10.75-ounce) can cream of chicken soup

1⅓ cups plus ¾ cup plus 1 tablespoon whole milk

1 tablespoon baking powder

½ teaspoon salt

4 tablespoons unsalted butter or butter-flavored shortening, cold, cut into small cubes

DIRECTIONS

1. Preheat the oven to 450°F and lightly coat a 9-inch deep-dish pie plate with cooking spray.

2. In a medium skillet, heat the oil over medium-high heat. Add the ham and cook for 1 minute, then add the onion and bell pepper and continue to cook until the vegetables are tender, for an additional 2 minutes. Add ¼ cup of the flour to the pan and stir for 1 minute to cook the flour, then add the soup and 1⅓ cups of the milk and stir until the mixture is thickened. Pour the mixture into the pie plate.

3. In a medium bowl, combine 2 cups of the flour, the baking powder, and salt and stir to mix well. Add the butter and mix with a fork or pastry cutter until the mixture resembles granola, then stir in ¾ cup of the milk until a soft dough forms.

4. Sprinkle a work surface with the remaining 1 tablespoon flour and turn the dough out onto it. Knead 2 or 3 times until the dough comes together smoothly. Use a rolling pin to roll to ½-inch thickness and cut with a biscuit or cookie cutter into 8 circles.

5. Place the dough rounds on top of the hot mixture in the pie plate and brush with the remaining 1 tablespoon milk. Bake for 18 to 20 minutes, until the filling is bubbling and the biscuits are nicely golden brown. Serve.

2

Appetizers and Side Dishes

If I could never cook a full meal again, I would be happy putting

together side dishes and arranging them on a countertop, encouraging

people to graze, try new things, and embrace variety. In this

chapter you will find a few of my favorite sides and appetizers,

which, when combined, can most certainly make a meal!

Party Popper Potato Puff Casserole

Yield: Serves 12 | Prep Time: 30 minutes | Cook Time: 40 minutes

On Tater Tot day in grade school, plates were piled high with golden nuggets and accompanied by mounds of salty-sweet ketchup. In hindsight, and in comparison to this casserole, that was a bland way to eat these magical potato pillows. Years later, I have found that the key is in the toppings. This party popper casserole gives the potatoes a kick with bacon, jalapeños, cheese, and more! Prep ahead of time and heat up when the kids get home from school or company arrives.

INGREDIENTS

2 pounds frozen potato puffs

1 pound cream cheese, room temperature

1 cup sour cream

2 cups shredded Mexican cheese blend

6 strips bacon, cooked and chopped

6 scallions, thinly sliced

5 jalapeño peppers, chopped

DIRECTIONS

1. Preheat the oven to 425°F and lightly coat a 9 × 13-inch baking dish with cooking spray.

2. Arrange the potato puffs evenly in the baking dish and bake for 15 minutes. In a medium bowl, stir together the cream cheese, sour cream, and 1½ cups of the shredded cheese. Add half the bacon, half the scallions, and the jalapeños. Spread the cheese mixture in a smooth layer over the potato puffs and top with the remaining shredded cheese, bacon, and scallions.

3. Bake for 20 to 25 minutes, until bubbling and the cheese has melted. Serve.

VARIATIONS

Do you love green peppers? Red onions? Add 'em! Customize your casserole with vegetables you love. Or try a flavored cream cheese, such as bacon.

Smoked Gouda Mac and Cheese

Yield: Serves 6 | Prep Time: 15 minutes | Cook Time: 40 minutes

Move aside, boxed mac and cheese; the new guy is in town. The smoky flavor from grated Gouda paired with salty bacon makes this a rich, creamy, and decadent pasta. Served as a side dish, an appetizer, or even a main course, this mac and cheese is unforgettable.

INGREDIENTS

1 teaspoon plus 5 tablespoons unsalted butter

1 pound cellentani (corkscrew pasta)

3 tablespoons all-purpose flour

3½ cups whole milk

3 cups shredded sharp white cheddar cheese

2 cups shredded smoked Gouda cheese

½ teaspoon dry mustard

½ teaspoon kosher salt

½ teaspoon freshly ground black pepper

¼ teaspoon ground nutmeg

1 cup panko bread crumbs

6 strips bacon, cooked and crumbled

Fresh parsley, for garnish

DIRECTIONS

1. Preheat the oven to 375°F and lightly coat a 9 × 13-inch baking dish with 1 teaspoon of the butter.

2. Bring a large pot of water to a boil. Add the cellentani and cook until al dente, then drain and return to the pot.

3. Melt 3 tablespoons of the butter in a large saucepan, then add the flour using a whisk and cook for 1 to 2 minutes, being careful not to burn it. Whisk in the milk and cook until the mixture thickens and coats the back of a wooden spoon.

4. Turn off the heat and add the cheeses, dry mustard, salt, pepper, and nutmeg. Stir until the cheeses have melted and all the ingredients are combined. Pour the cheese sauce into the pot with the pasta and mix well. Pour into the baking dish.

5. In a small skillet, melt the remaining 2 tablespoons butter over medium heat, add the panko, and cook until slightly brown. Sprinkle the crumb mixture on top of the casserole and bake for 30 minutes until bubbling hot and golden. Sprinkle with the bacon, garnish with parsley, and serve.

NOTES

Any short pasta shape will work, although I particularly love the curly shape of the cellentani.

No-Fuss Root Vegetable Casserole

Yield: Serves 6 to 8 | Prep Time: 1 hour | Cook Time: 1 hour 30 minutes

When you think of root vegetables, you might think difficult and even fussy. But these aren't! First of all, I like potato skins (and you may, too; they're packed with flavor), so I skip peeling my potatoes. The other vegetables are quick to peel and roast just as fast. The best thing about this casserole is that it can be made ahead of time and reheated in the oven when you're ready to serve. So when entertaining a crowd, you can make it in the morning, or even the night before.

INGREDIENTS

1 celery root, peeled

3 parsnips, peeled

1 large sweet potato, unpeeled

2 to 3 russet potatoes, unpeeled

1 red onion

1 tablespoon olive oil

1 tablespoon fresh thyme leaves

1 teaspoon salt

½ teaspoon freshly ground black pepper

2 tablespoons unsalted butter

3 garlic cloves, slivered

3 cups heavy cream

2 bay leaves

1 cup shredded cheddar cheese

½ cup grated Parmesan cheese

Rosemary sprigs, for garnish

DIRECTIONS

1. Preheat the oven to 400°F. Line 2 large baking sheets with foil and spray with cooking spray. Lightly coat a 9 × 13-inch baking dish with cooking spray and set aside.

2. Cut the celery root, parsnips, sweet potato, russet potatoes, and red onion into a uniform, large dice and place in a large bowl. Add the olive oil, thyme, salt, and pepper and toss to coat. Arrange the vegetables on the baking sheets in a single layer and bake for 45 minutes, turning halfway through the baking time. Remove the vegetables and lower the oven temperature to 350°F.

3. While the vegetables roast, melt the butter in a small saucepan over medium heat, add the garlic, and cook for 1 minute, until fragrant. Add the cream and bay leaves and bring to a low simmer, then remove from the heat and allow the flavors to steep, about 10 minutes.

4. Layer half of the vegetables into the baking dish. Top with half of the cheddar cheese and then add the remaining vegetables in an even layer on top. Remove the bay leaves from the steeped cream and pour the mixture over the vegetables.

5. Sprinkle the remaining cheddar and the Parmesan cheese over the casserole and bake for 45 minutes, until the top is golden brown. Garnish with rosemary sprigs and serve.

Green Bean Casserole

Yield: Serves 10 to 12 | Prep Time: 25 minutes | Cook Time: 30 minutes

If I'm being honest, green beans aren't my favorite vegetable. I never ate them growing up, sticking instead to corn (from our farm), potatoes, and frozen peas. So my casually ignoring green beans turned into a dislike of them. But they sure are good for you. How, I wondered, could I find a way to make them a part of my diet? Well, I will tell you that coating them in a creamy mushroom sauce and topping them with caramelized onions works. No longer will you need to trick the kiddos (or me) into eating a green bean!

INGREDIENTS

2 pounds green beans, trimmed

4 tablespoons olive oil

1 yellow onion, finely chopped

1 cup grated Parmesan cheese

½ cup dried bread crumbs

½ teaspoon salt

½ teaspoon freshly ground black pepper

1 pound white button mushrooms, sliced

6 garlic cloves, minced

3 tablespoons all-purpose flour

1 cup whole milk

½ cup vegetable broth

DIRECTIONS

1. Preheat the oven to 375°F. Bring a large pot of salted water to a boil. Add the green beans and cook for 5 minutes. Drain the beans and place them in a 9 × 13-inch baking dish sprayed with cooking spray.

2. Meanwhile, in a large skillet, heat 2 tablespoons of the olive oil over medium heat, add the onion, and sauté until golden. Add ½ cup of the Parmesan, the bread crumbs, salt, and pepper.

3. In a medium saucepan, heat the remaining 2 tablespoons oil over medium heat, add the mushrooms and garlic, and sauté for 2 minutes. Add the flour and cook, stirring, for another 2 minutes. Add the milk and broth and cook, stirring, until thickened.

4. Pour the mushroom sauce over the green beans. Top with the onion mixture and bake for 25 minutes, until warm and golden brown. Serve.

Zoodle (Mock Noodle) Casserole

Yield: Serves 2 | Prep Time: 10 minutes | Cook Time: 25 minutes

If you love noodles but want to cut down on the carbs, these zoodles have such a striking resemblance that you'll forget you're eating anything other than your favorite pasta. The first time I discovered zoodles was at a tiny restaurant below my apartment in Manhattan. I would meet one of my best friends there for dinner. We lived on opposite sides of the city, and if you know and love Manhattan, you know that someone going from the Lower East Side to an Upper West Side restaurant is not so convenient. That said, she made the trek because of these zoodles. Ever since, I've wanted to replicate the recipe at home and this version does just that. The zucchini soaks up the sauce and cheese, resulting in a great weeknight dinner.

INGREDIENTS

4 zucchini

1 (28-ounce) jar marinara sauce

1 cup grated Parmesan cheese

1 teaspoon salt

½ teaspoon freshly ground black pepper

DIRECTIONS

1. Preheat the oven to 375°F and lightly coat an 8 × 8-inch baking dish with cooking spray.

2. Using a spiralizer, turn the zucchini into zoodles with a medium thickness.

3. Toss the zoodles with the marinara sauce, cheese, salt, and pepper and transfer to the baking dish. Bake for 25 minutes, until warm and bubbling. Serve.

Broccoli-Bacon Casserole

Yield: Serves 6 | Prep Time: 15 minutes | Cook Time: 30 minutes

If you're looking to add a little green to your diet, this is the way to do it. Blanched broccoli combined with cheese sauce and bacon is one of my favorite side dishes to serve with chicken or beef.

INGREDIENTS

6 cups broccoli florets

8 ounces cream cheese, room temperature

4 scallions, sliced

2 tablespoons whole milk

1 teaspoon garlic powder

1½ cups shredded cheddar cheese

10 strips bacon, cooked and chopped

DIRECTIONS

1. Preheat the oven to 425°F. Bring a large pot of salted water to a boil. Add the broccoli and cook for 2 minutes. Drain.

2. In a large bowl, combine the cream cheese, scallions, milk, and garlic powder. Add the broccoli and stir until coated. Place the broccoli mixture in an 8 × 8-inch baking dish.

3. Top with the cheese and bacon and cover with foil. Bake for 25 minutes. Remove the foil and continue baking for 5 minutes, until slightly golden. Serve.

NOTES

You can substitute a 2.5-ounce box of precooked bacon for the bacon in this recipe.

Cheesy Corn Casserole

Yield: Serves 4 | Prep Time: 10 minutes | Cook Time: 55 minutes

I have a lot of memories of growing up on a family farm, most of them including food—and not just in the kitchen, but in other ways. We took turns riding the combine with my grandfather: that giant green tractor that combed through the corn rows and tossed full stalks in the back. We kids were in charge of shucking the corn for dinner. I remember sitting on the front steps of the farmhouse, and the sound of the green corn husks sliding off to reveal little gold kernels. If you like cornbread and you like creamed corn, this is the ultimate side dish. With only 10 minutes of prep, you won't even break a sweat, unlike me in my days of shucking.

INGREDIENTS

2 (15.25-ounce) cans whole kernel corn, drained

1 (14.75-ounce) can cream-style corn

1 (8-ounce) box corn muffin mix

4 ounces cream cheese, room temperature

½ cup sour cream

2 large eggs

8 tablespoons unsalted butter, melted

4 scallions, thinly sliced

1½ cups shredded white cheddar cheese

Chopped fresh cilantro

Salt and freshly ground black pepper

DIRECTIONS

1. Preheat the oven to 350°F and lightly coat a 9 × 13-inch baking dish, two mini loaf pans, or four 6-ounce ramekins with cooking spray.

2. In a large bowl, combine 1 can of the whole kernel corn, the creamed corn, muffin mix, cream cheese, sour cream, eggs, melted butter, and scallions and mix well.

3. Pour the batter into the baking dish or ramekins and bake for 45 minutes, until set.

4. Remove from the oven, top with the cheese, and bake for an additional 5 to 10 minutes, until the cheese has melted. Sprinkle with the remaining can of corn, cilantro, salt, and pepper, and serve.

Double-Loaded Potato Casserole

Yield: Serves 4 to 6 | Prep Time: 15 minutes | Cook Time: 1½ hours

This is a simple yet elegant and easy way to serve potatoes. No matter the occasion, this take on potato gratin is beautiful, creamy, and easy to serve. Don't worry about peeling the potatoes; their salty roasted skins just add to the flavor.

INGREDIENTS

3 russet potatoes, unpeeled

½ teaspoon salt

½ teaspoon freshly ground black pepper

½ cup shredded Asiago cheese

½ cup shredded Monterey Jack cheese

8 strips bacon, cooked and crumbled

1 cup whole milk

1 large egg

Chopped fresh thyme

DIRECTIONS

1. Preheat the oven to 375°F and lightly coat a 9-inch pie plate with cooking spray.

2. Using a mandoline or knife, slice the potatoes ¼ inch thick. Spread half of the potatoes in the pie plate and season with the salt and pepper. Sprinkle half of each cheese and then the bacon over the potatoes and add the remaining potato slices. Top with the remaining cheese.

3. In a small bowl, combine the milk and egg. Pour over the potatoes. Cover the dish with foil and bake for 1½ hours. Sprinkle with thyme and serve.

Best-Ever Butternut Squash Casserole

Yield: Serves 6 | Prep Time: 20 minutes | Cook Time: 1¾ hours

If you're looking for a new way to eat squash, look no further. My first job after culinary school and working in France was with Daniel Boulud. I began at his restaurant group working in *garde-manger*, the salad and appetizer station, and I spent a lot of time making soup, much of which was butternut squash soup. I found that if you pop a squash in the microwave, it will soften the outer layer and make it easier to slice, and that patience is a must when roasting and pureeing. This casserole takes the flavors and techniques that I used back then to create an easier squash dish. You'll love the taste of this sweet vegetable in a fun new form.

INGREDIENTS

3 pounds butternut squash

1 tablespoon olive oil

6 garlic cloves, minced

3 sprigs fresh thyme, removed from stem

1 teaspoon salt

1 teaspoon freshly ground black pepper

3 large eggs

2 tablespoons all-purpose flour

1¼ cups half-and-half

2 tablespoons unsalted butter

10 fresh sage leaves

NOTES

To make slicing the squash easier, microwave the whole squash for 3 minutes—this will soften the outer layer enough to make it easier and safer to slice.

DIRECTIONS

1. Preheat the oven to 375°F and lightly coat a 9-inch deep-dish pie plate with cooking spray. Line a baking sheet with aluminum foil.

2. Peel and then slice the butternut squash into large cubes, place on the foil-lined baking sheet, and drizzle with the olive oil. Sprinkle garlic, thyme, ½ teaspoon salt, and ½ teaspoon pepper on top. Bake for 45 minutes, until the squash is tender. Remove the squash and lower the oven temperature to 350°F.

3. Meanwhile, whisk the eggs and flour in a medium bowl to make a thick, smooth mixture. Whisk in the half-and-half and the remaining salt and pepper and set aside.

4. Combine the squash with the egg mixture and pour into the pie plate. Bake for 1 hour, until golden brown and the center is completely cooked and jiggles slightly.

5. In a small saucepan, melt the butter over medium-low heat and cook until it has just begun to turn brown—watch closely so it does not burn. Drop in the sage leaves and let them sizzle and crisp. Pour the melted butter and scatter the sage leaves over the squash. Serve.

Holiday Sweet Potato Casserole

Yield: Serves 8 to 10 | Prep Time: 1 hour | Cook Time: 1 hour 15 minutes

Did you know that marshmallows have magical invisibility powers? The reason we wait until the very end of the baking time to add marshmallows to a casserole is that if they're baked slightly over the toasted browning phase, they will disappear! Yes, vanish. There is a minute or so when they are perfectly golden brown, and if you miss that minute—poof!—the ooey-gooey marshmallows explode. This isn't a bad thing; they will coat the top of these delicious sweet potatoes either way. But try it for yourself and see what you think.

INGREDIENTS

6 sweet potatoes

1 cup granulated sugar

4 tablespoons unsalted butter, melted

½ cup whole milk

2 large eggs

Streusel Topping

1 cup light brown sugar

1 cup pecans, chopped

½ cup all-purpose flour

4 tablespoons unsalted butter, melted

1 to 2 cups mini marshmallows

DIRECTIONS

1. Preheat the oven to 425°F and line a baking sheet with aluminum foil. Pierce the sweet potatoes with a fork, place them on the baking sheet, and bake until tender, about 45 minutes. Remove the potatoes and lower the oven temperature to 350°F.

2. Meanwhile, combine all the topping ingredients except for the marshmallows in a small bowl.

3. Peel the potatoes and mash them with the sugar, 4 tablespoons butter, milk, and eggs. Pour the mixture into a 9-inch pie plate. Sprinkle the topping over the potatoes and bake for 20 minutes. Remove from the oven and add the marshmallows. Add at least 1 cup and up to 2 cups depending on how sweet you want the casserole to be. Bake for an additional 10 minutes. Serve.

French Onion Soup Casserole

Yield: Serves 6 to 8 | Prep Time: 30 minutes | Cook Time: 55 minutes

When people ask what is my favorite thing to cook, I usually say it's something that lets me stand over the stove and stir, but then allows me to leave it behind and socialize. This dish is a good example of just that. I love the act of sautéing the onions and garlic, watching the butter melt, and patiently waiting as the onions decide to brown. At just the right time, when my guests arrive and I want to step away from the stove, this casserole is ready to be poured into a pan and baked. It's a sit-by-the-fire, read-a-book, and snuggle-up kind of casserole, one that I hope you enjoy as much as I do.

INGREDIENTS

2 tablespoons unsalted butter

3 large yellow onions, thinly sliced

¼ teaspoon sugar

1¼ cups chicken broth

1½ cups beef broth

1 teaspoon chopped fresh thyme

1 teaspoon Dijon mustard

½ teaspoon kosher salt

½ teaspoon freshly ground black pepper

1 baguette, sliced ½ inch thick (24 slices)

2 cups shredded Gruyère cheese

Fresh thyme, for garnish

DIRECTIONS

1. Preheat the oven to 350°F and lightly coat a 9 × 13-inch baking dish with cooking spray. Line a baking sheet with parchment paper.

2. In a large saucepan, melt the butter over medium heat. Add the onions and cook, stirring occasionally, until the onions are soft and golden. Halfway through the cooking, around 2 minutes, add the sugar to help the onions caramelize. When the onions are done, add the chicken and beef broths, thyme, mustard, salt, and pepper. Simmer for 5 to 10 minutes.

3. Place the bread slices on the parchment-lined baking sheet and toast 2 to 3 minutes on each side.

4. Place half of the bread slices in the baking dish, overlapping slightly.

5. Layer half of the onion mixture on top of the bread slices. Top with remaining bread slices, then the remaining onion mixture. Cover with the cheese. Cover with foil and bake until hot and bubbling, 30 to 35 minutes. Garnish with fresh thyme and serve.

Perfect Pizza Casserole

Yield: Serves 6 to 8 | Prep Time: 20 minutes | Cook Time: 30 minutes

Pizza meets pie meets casserole in this quick and easy recipe. Layer meat, marinara, and cheese and top with a baking mix crust for a fun, perfect pizza that is even easier than delivery.

INGREDIENTS

1 cup baking mix

½ cup whole milk

2 large eggs, beaten

1 cup shredded mozzarella cheese

12 ounces Italian sausage, mild or hot

1 onion, diced

1 (14-ounce) can pizza sauce

4 ounces pepperoni, thinly sliced

Crushed red pepper flakes (optional)

DIRECTIONS

1. Preheat the oven to 400°F and lightly coat a 9-inch pie plate with cooking spray.

2. In a medium bowl, stir together the baking mix, milk, and eggs just until combined and doughy. Stir in ½ cup of the mozzarella cheese and press the mixture into the bottom of the pie plate.

3. In a large skillet, begin cooking the sausage with the casings removed over medium heat, stirring to break up the meat. Add the onion and cook until the meat is browned, about 5 minutes. Drain off any excess fat and return to the heat. Stir in the pizza sauce until just heated and beginning to bubble. Pour into the pie plate and top with the pepperoni slices and the remaining ½ cup of cheese.

4. Bake for 25 minutes. Allow to set for 20 minutes. Remove from pie plate, if desired, top with crushed red pepper flakes, slice, and serve.

Nacho Cheese Chip Casserole

Yield: Serves 8 | Prep Time: 15 minutes | Cook Time: 30 minutes

What makes a nacho cheese chip so good? Is it the color? The orange powder that packs a punch of flavor, or that triangle shape? I would argue it's all of that. I did my fair share of salty snack eating and chip designing when I worked at gravitytank, an innovation consulting firm. I was a culinary designer, so my job was to come up with new snack ideas for companies, large and small, and create edible prototypes of these concepts for people to taste. You'd think by now I would have had enough! But when given the opportunity to try these cheesy chips on top of a ground beef skillet casserole it was too tempting not to, and I am sure glad that I did.

INGREDIENTS

8 ounces rigatoni

1 teaspoon salt

2 tablespoons olive oil

1 pound lean ground beef

1 (1-ounce) packet taco seasoning

1 onion, diced

1 cup canned whole kernel corn, drained

1 cup prepared salsa

½ cup water

1 (15.5-ounce) bag nacho cheese chips, all but ½ cup crushed

1½ cups shredded Mexican cheese blend

DIRECTIONS

1. Preheat the oven to 350°F and lightly coat a 9 × 13-inch baking dish with cooking spray.

2. Bring a large pot of water to a boil, add the rigatoni and the salt, and cook until al dente. Drain and reserve.

3. In a large skillet, heat the olive oil over medium-high heat, add the beef and the taco seasoning, and cook for 4 minutes. Stir in the onion and continue to cook for another 3 minutes, until the meat is completely cooked. Add the corn, salsa, and water and continue to cook until hot and bubbling. Add the cooked rigatoni and remove from heat.

4. Set aside ½ cup of the uncrushed chips, then spread about half of the remaining chips in the bottom of the baking dish and top with half of the meat mixture. Add half of the cheese. Repeat with the remaining crushed chips, meat mixture, and cheese. Bake for 20 minutes to heat through and melt the cheese. Sprinkle the reserved uncrushed chips over the top and serve.

3

Chicken

Chicken is my go-to protein. When I'm planning a meal, it is a great

canvas to start with. With its neutral flavor, you can season and prepare

chicken in many different ways. This allows me to be creative any

day of the week, while feeling good about what goes on the table.

Potato Chip and Chicken Casserole

Yield: Serves 6 | Prep Time: 15 minutes | Cook Time: 30 minutes

The name got you, didn't it? If you have ever put potato chips in a sandwich, you're already on my level. They almost act like a new form of salt—crunchy and texturally exciting. It's a perfect topping for one of my favorite cheesy chicken casseroles.

INGREDIENTS

2 cups shredded cooked chicken breast meat

1 (5.5-ounce) bag chicken and broccoli rice side

1 (10.75-ounce) can cream of chicken soup

1 (10.75-ounce) can cream of celery soup

1 red bell pepper, sliced

Juice from 1 lemon

1 cup shredded cheddar cheese

1 (10.5-ounce) bag wavy potato chips

DIRECTIONS

1. Preheat the oven to 400°F and lightly coat a 9 × 13-inch baking dish with cooking spray.

2. Combine the chicken, rice side, both soups, bell pepper, and lemon juice in a large bowl and pour into the baking dish. Sprinkle the cheese and potato chips evenly over the top and bake for 30 minutes. Serve.

NOTES

To cook the chicken, place 2 medium boneless, skinless chicken breasts on a baking sheet and bake at 350°F for 30 minutes. Remove from the oven and shred.

Country Chicken and Spinach Casserole

Yield: Serves 4 | Prep Time: 20 minutes | Cook Time: 20 minutes

What a dish! It sort of looks like a salad, but believe me—this is no salad. Packed with cheese, this spinach and chicken combo is creamy and to die for, similar to spinach dip. Topped with torn toasted bread and baked until bubbling hot, this will be a family favorite.

INGREDIENTS

2 tablespoons unsalted butter

1 onion, diced

4 garlic cloves, minced

¼ cup dry white wine

1½ cups heavy cream

2 tablespoons all-purpose flour

8 ounces baby spinach

2 cups shredded cooked chicken breast meat

1 teaspoon salt

1 teaspoon freshly ground black pepper

2 cups torn challah bread

DIRECTIONS

1. Preheat the oven to 450°F. Coat an 8-inch round baking dish with cooking spray.

2. In a large saucepan, melt 1 tablespoon of the butter over medium heat. Add the onion and garlic and sauté for 5 minutes. Add the wine and continue to sauté for an additional 5 minutes. Add the cream and the flour. Bring to a boil and stir continuously. Remove from the heat and add the spinach, chicken, salt, and pepper. Place the mixture in the baking dish and top with the torn challah. Melt the remaining butter and pour it over the bread. Bake for 10 minutes, until golden brown. Serve.

NOTES

To cook the chicken, place 2 medium boneless, skinless chicken breasts on a baking sheet and bake at 350°F for 30 minutes. Remove from the oven and shred.

Chicken Divan Casserole

Yield: Serves 8 | Prep Time: 25 minutes | Cook Time: 1 hour

I love traveling, particularly to other countries, and finding small boutique hotels to stay in. Whether at a hotel bar, on a velvet couch in a lounge, or in a place that has hot coffee and Wi-Fi, my husband and I naturally look for places to gather with friends or family. This chicken dish, topped with almonds and broccoli, is a memorable dish no matter where we go.

INGREDIENTS

1 pound broccoli florets and stems, chopped

2 tablespoons olive oil

1 onion, diced

1½ cups white rice

4 tablespoons unsalted butter plus 2 tablespoons, melted

¼ cup all-purpose flour

¾ cup heavy cream

1 teaspoon Dijon mustard

½ teaspoon salt

1½ cups shredded cheddar or Monterey Jack cheese

4 cups chicken breasts, cooked and shredded

½ cup dried bread crumbs

½ cup chopped almonds

NOTES

To cook the chicken, place 4 boneless, skinless chicken breasts on a baking sheet and bake at 350°F for 30 minutes. Remove from the oven and shred.

DIRECTIONS

1. Preheat the oven to 400°F and lightly coat a 9 × 13-inch baking dish with cooking spray. Bring a large pot of salted water to a boil and cook the broccoli for 5 minutes. Drain, reserving 1 cup of the liquid, and set broccoli and liquid aside.

2. In a large saucepan, heat the olive oil over medium-high heat. Add the onion and cooked broccoli and sauté, stirring, until the onion is translucent. Add the rice and 3 cups water and bring to a boil. Cover and simmer for 15 minutes (the rice may not be completely cooked but will cook further in the oven).

3. In a medium saucepan, melt 4 tablespoons butter over medium heat. Add the flour and cook, stirring, for 1 full minute until the mixture is beginning to color. Add 1 cup of the set-aside cooking liquid and stir until the sauce becomes creamy and thick. Add the cream and cook until the mixture is thick enough to coat a spoon. Remove from the heat, add the mustard and salt, then stir in the cheese until it is melted.

4. Spread the rice mixture into a smooth layer in the bottom of the baking dish. Add the broccoli around the edges, then arrange the chicken pieces in the center of the dish. Pour the sauce over all, leaving the broccoli florets peeking through.

5. Combine the bread crumbs, almonds, and the 2 tablespoons melted butter in a small bowl. Sprinkle over the casserole and bake for 30 to 35 minutes, until bubbling and lightly browned. Serve.

Unforgettable Buffalo Chicken Casserole

Yield: Serves 6 to 8 | Prep Time: 15 minutes | Cook Time: 45 minutes

I can't count on my hands how many times my husband has asked for this casserole, not only when we entertain, but also on any given weeknight. Potatoes, chicken, cheese, and bacon—that foursome is indeed unforgettable, and when I make this at home on a weekend, I set the scene for our own little sports bar.

INGREDIENTS

Chicken Filling

⅓ cup olive oil

5 tablespoons hot sauce

1 tablespoon smoked paprika

1 tablespoon finely minced garlic

2 teaspoons freshly ground black pepper

1 teaspoon salt

2 pounds Yukon gold potatoes, unpeeled, cut into cubes

2 pounds boneless, skinless chicken breasts, cut into 1-inch cubes

Topping

2 cups shredded cheddar cheese

6 strips bacon, cooked and crumbled

8 scallions, sliced

½ cup chopped celery

DIRECTIONS

1. Preheat the oven to 450°F and lightly coat a 9 × 13-inch baking dish with cooking spray.

2. For the chicken filling: In a large bowl, mix the olive oil, hot sauce, paprika, garlic, pepper, and salt. Add the potatoes and mix well to coat. Using a slotted spoon, remove the potatoes from the bowl (but don't wash out the bowl yet!). Place the potatoes in the baking dish and bake for 25 minutes, until the potatoes are almost tender and beginning to crisp. While the potatoes bake, add the chicken to the bowl with the spice mixture and toss well.

3. For the topping: Mix the topping ingredients together in a medium bowl.

4. Remove the potatoes from the oven and lower the oven temperature to 400°F. Stir the potatoes and place the uncooked chicken cubes on top in an even layer. Sprinkle with the topping mixture and bake for 20 minutes, until the cheese is melted. Serve.

King Ranch Barbeque Chicken Casserole

Yield: Serves 8 | Prep Time: 30 minutes | Cook Time: 50 minutes

When I think of dinnertime on a ranch, I think cast-iron skillet and corn chips. Sitting around a campfire with a horse in the background, eating something barbequed. This casserole has beans, chicken, smoky sauce, and a salty corn chip topping. Named after one of the greatest ranches in Texas, this casserole is as big as it is bold.

INGREDIENTS

5 tablespoons olive or vegetable oil

1 tablespoon chili powder

1 tablespoon cayenne pepper

1 teaspoon salt

½ tablespoon ground cumin

2 pounds boneless, skinless chicken thighs, cut into 1-inch cubes

1 cup diced onion

1 cup diced green bell pepper

2 garlic cloves, finely minced

8 ounces cheddar, sliced

8 (6-inch) corn tortillas, cut into quarters

1 (10.75-ounce) can cream of chicken soup

1 (10.75-ounce) can cheddar cheese soup

1 (10-ounce) can tomatoes with chiles

1 cup shredded Mexican cheese blend

2 cups corn chips

DIRECTIONS

1. Preheat the oven to 375°F and lightly coat a deep 9 × 13-inch baking dish with cooking spray.

2. In a large bowl, combine 3 tablespoons of the oil with the chili powder, cayenne, salt, and cumin and stir to moisten the spices completely. Add the chicken and toss to coat.

3. In a deep 10-inch skillet, heat the remaining 2 tablespoons oil over medium heat. Add the onions, bell pepper, and garlic, and sauté, stirring, for 10 minutes. Add the chicken, cover, and cook for 10 minutes, stirring once or twice.

4. Layer half of the chicken, half of the cheddar, and half of the tortilla pieces in the baking dish; repeat. In a bowl, combine the soups and tomatoes and pour over the casserole. Bake for 20 minutes. Top with the shredded cheese and the corn chips and bake for an additional 5 to 10 minutes, until bubbling. Serve.

Butter Cracker Chicken Casserole

Yield: Serves 6 to 8 | Prep Time: 15 minutes | Cook Time: 30 minutes

A classic, retro chicken casserole from the '50s with butter crackers and cream of celery soup combines just the right stuff. I took that classic dish and added a tangy twist with Greek yogurt.

INGREDIENTS

2 pounds boneless, skinless chicken breasts, cooked and shredded

1 (10.75-ounce) can cream of celery soup

1 cup plain Greek yogurt

1 cup finely chopped celery, including some of the leaves

6 scallions, sliced

½ teaspoon freshly ground black pepper

2½ cups butter cracker crumbs

4 tablespoons unsalted butter, melted

DIRECTIONS

1. Preheat the oven to 350°F and lightly spray a 9 × 13-inch baking dish with cooking spray.

2. In a large bowl, combine the chicken, soup, yogurt, celery, scallions, and pepper. Stir to mix well, then spoon into the baking dish. Sprinkle with the cracker crumbs and drizzle with the melted butter. Bake for about 30 minutes, until the casserole is bubbling and the top is golden brown. Serve.

NOTES

To cook the chicken, place the breasts on a baking sheet and bake at 350°F for 30 minutes. Remove from the oven and shred.

Everyday Chicken Parmesan Casserole

Yield: Serves 6 to 8 | Prep Time: 20 minutes | Cook Time: 25 minutes

This is one of the easiest things to make, yet completely worthy of a special date. Combine your ingredients, light some candles, and voilà, you have just set the scene for an Italian dinner at home. I serve this with a warm loaf of bread, a little salted butter and, of course, a glass of red wine. It's not a meal to turn down!

INGREDIENTS

4 cups shredded cooked chicken breast meat

1 (28-ounce) jar marinara sauce

8 ounces mozzarella cheese, sliced thin or shredded

½ cup grated Parmesan cheese

1 cup panko bread crumbs

2 tablespoons unsalted butter, melted

½ teaspoon salt

¼ teaspoon freshly ground black pepper

¼ teaspoon crushed red pepper flakes

2 teaspoons thinly sliced fresh basil

DIRECTIONS

1. Preheat the oven to 350°F and lightly coat an 8 × 8-inch baking dish with cooking spray.

2. Layer the chicken in the bottom of the baking dish. Pour the marinara over the chicken and stir to combine. Top with the mozzarella and Parmesan. In a small bowl, mix the panko with the melted butter, salt, pepper, and pepper flakes and sprinkle on top. Bake for 20 to 25 minutes, until bubbling and golden. Scatter the basil over the casserole and serve.

NOTES

To cook the chicken, place 4 boneless, skinless chicken breasts on a baking sheet and bake at 350°F for 30 minutes. Remove from the oven and shred.

One-Pot Chicken Cordon Bleu Casserole

Yield: Serves 6 to 8 | Prep Time: 20 minutes | Cook Time: 20 minutes

My husband and I are both from Minnesota, and when we head home for the holidays, one of our first stops is at a local restaurant for lunch. They no longer have chicken cordon bleu on the menu, but somehow he is able to order it anyway! With plenty of chicken, ham, cheese, and crispy bread crumbs to mimic the pan-fried classic, I've made one of our favorite meals a regular indulgence in this one-pot-wonder version.

INGREDIENTS

2 tablespoons olive oil

½ cup chopped onion

2 tablespoons all-purpose flour

1 cup chicken broth

½ cup whole milk

1 cup shredded Swiss cheese

2 cups shredded cooked chicken breast meat

2 cups cooked long-grain white or brown rice

8 ounces cooked ham steak, diced

½ cup panko bread crumbs

¼ cup shredded Parmesan cheese

1 tablespoon unsalted butter, melted

DIRECTIONS

1. Preheat the oven to 400°F.

2. In a deep 10-inch ovenproof and table-worthy skillet, heat the olive oil over medium heat, add the onion, and sauté for 1 minute, until translucent. Add the flour and stir for 1 minute until it turns golden brown. Gradually add the broth, whisking until thick and smooth, about 1 minute. Add the milk and whisk until the sauce is smooth, an additional minute. Remove from the heat and stir in the Swiss cheese until it is melted and incorporated.

3. Stir the chicken, rice, and ham into the sauce in the pan, mixing completely. Smooth the top. In a small bowl, combine the panko and Parmesan and stir in the melted butter, then sprinkle the mixture evenly over the top of the casserole. Bake for about 20 minutes, until the edges are bubbling and the top is lightly browned. Serve.

NOTES

To cook the chicken, place 2 boneless, skinless breasts on a baking sheet and bake at 350°F for 30 minutes. Remove from the oven and shred.

Hot Chicken Casserole

Yield: Serves 6 to 8 | Prep Time: 10 minutes | Cook Time: 45 minutes

A staple in our home, hot chicken casserole is fantastic for dinner and days after. Try it on toasted bread, atop romaine lettuce, or on a tortilla. No matter how you serve it or eat it, this casserole is primed to become a go-to in your weeknight rotation!

INGREDIENTS

3 cups chopped cooked chicken breast meat

1 cup cooked long-grain white rice

3 large hard-cooked eggs, chopped

½ cup chopped onion

1 (10.75-ounce) can cream of chicken soup

1 cup grated cheddar cheese

¾ cup mayonnaise

1 tablespoon lemon juice

Freshly ground black pepper

DIRECTIONS

1. Preheat the oven to 350°F. Lightly coat a 9 × 13-inch baking dish with cooking spray.

2. In a large bowl, stir together the chicken, rice, eggs, and onion. Stir in the soup, cheese, mayonnaise, and lemon juice. Season with black pepper. Spoon the chicken mixture into the baking dish. Bake for 45 minutes until bubbling. Serve.

NOTES

To cook the chicken, place 3 boneless, skinless chicken breasts on a baking sheet and bake at 350°F for 30 minutes. Remove from the oven and chop.

Country Comfort Chicken Casserole

Yield: Serves 6 to 8 | Prep Time: 20 minutes | Cook Time: 40 minutes

I love the texture of fusilli noodles. The little spiral grooves are ideal for holding sauce and, when tossed with chicken and hot cheese sauce, they are some of the most comforting noodles around. This warm and cozy casserole is a countryside classic.

INGREDIENTS

14 ounces fusilli

Salt and freshly ground black pepper

1 tablespoon olive oil

1 (10.75-ounce) can cheddar cheese soup

1 cup sour cream

½ cup shredded cheddar cheese

1 teaspoon dried basil

2 cups chopped cooked chicken breast meat

3 tablespoons Italian-style bread crumbs

2 tablespoons chopped fresh parsley

2 tablespoons unsalted butter, melted

Fresh thyme, for garnish (optional)

DIRECTIONS

1. Preheat the oven to 350°F and lightly coat a 9 × 9-inch baking dish with cooking spray.

2. Bring a large pot of water to a boil, add the fusilli and 1 teaspoon salt, and cook until al dente. Drain and toss with the olive oil.

3. In a large bowl, combine the soup, sour cream, cheese, and basil and season with salt and pepper to taste. Stir in the chicken and cooked fusilli. Spoon into the baking dish. Mix the bread crumbs and parsley and sprinkle on top, then drizzle with the melted butter. Bake for 30 minutes, until hot and bubbling. Serve, garnished with fresh thyme if desired.

NOTES

To cook the chicken, place 2 boneless, skinless chicken breasts on a baking sheet and bake at 350°F for 30 minutes. Remove from the oven and chop.

Amish Chicken Casserole

Yield: Serves 6 to 8 | Prep Time: 20 minutes | Cook Time: 45 minutes

Amish-style cooking has a good reputation, for good reason. With sizable gardens and home-raised livestock, the Amish take a home-grown, fresh, and simple—yet delightful—approach to meals. Peas and mushrooms combined with egg noodles and chicken are a perfect example of the simplicity of a meal that celebrates fresh produce and focuses on each individual ingredient.

INGREDIENTS

8 ounces medium egg noodles

2 teaspoons salt

8 tablespoons unsalted butter

½ cup all-purpose flour

2 cups chicken broth

1 cup whole milk

½ teaspoon freshly ground black pepper

½ teaspoon poultry seasoning

2 cups shredded or chopped cooked chicken breast meat

8 ounces button mushrooms, sliced

1 cup frozen peas, thawed

⅓ cup chopped onion

2 tablespoons chopped fresh parsley

DIRECTIONS

1. Preheat the oven to 350°F and lightly coat a 9 × 13-inch baking dish with cooking spray.

2. Bring a large pot of water to a boil, add the noodles and 1 teaspoon of the salt, and cook until al dente; drain and reserve.

3. While the noodles are cooking, melt the butter in a medium saucepan over medium heat, stir in the flour, and cook for 1 full minute, until the mixture is beginning to color. Add the broth and stir until the sauce becomes creamy and thickens. Add the milk and cook, stirring for an additional minute. Season with the remaining 1 teaspoon salt, the pepper, and the poultry seasoning.

4. In a large bowl, stir together the chicken, mushrooms, peas, onion, and parsley. Add the noodles and sauce and toss well to coat. Spoon into the baking dish. Bake for 30 minutes until bubbling and golden brown. Serve.

NOTES

To cook the chicken, place 2 boneless, skinless chicken breasts on a baking sheet and bake at 350°F for 30 minutes. Remove from the oven and shred.

Golden Mushroom and Chicken Skillet Casserole

Yield: Serves 6 to 8 | Prep Time: 20 minutes | Cook Time: 45 minutes

When sautéed in butter with onions, salt, and pepper, mushrooms shrink down and turn golden as they soak up every ounce of goodness. The taste shines through in this cheesy chicken casserole, and the comforting smell will fill your home.

INGREDIENTS

1 tablespoon sweet paprika

1 teaspoon salt

½ teaspoon freshly ground black pepper

¼ teaspoon ground nutmeg

2 pounds boneless, skinless chicken breasts, sliced 2 inches thick

1 tablespoon unsalted butter

2 cups thinly sliced onions

1 pound cremini mushrooms, halved

¾ cup white wine

2 cups chicken broth

2 bay leaves

1 (10.75-ounce) can cream of mushroom soup

¼ cup half-and-half

6 servings instant mashed potatoes

Fresh parsley, chopped, for garnish

DIRECTIONS

1. In a large bowl, combine the paprika, salt, pepper, and nutmeg. Add the chicken and toss until the meat is well coated.

2. In a large, deep skillet, heat the butter over medium-high heat. Add the chicken and sauté until lightly browned, about 3 minutes per side. (The chicken may not be completely cooked through but will finish in the final step.) Transfer the chicken to a plate.

3. Add the onions to the pan and cook, stirring, until tender. Add the mushrooms and sauté for 5 minutes. Pour in the wine and stir to lift any browned bits from the pan. Continue to cook until the wine is reduced by half. Add the chicken broth and bay leaves and stir, then add the soup and stir until smooth. Return the chicken to the pan, cover, and lower the heat to medium-low so that the liquid just bubbles around the edges. Cook for 30 minutes.

4. Remove the lid, remove the bay leaves, and stir in the half-and-half. Sprinkle with fresh parsley. Serve the chicken and its gravy with the mashed potatoes.

Chicken Pot Pie Casserole

Yield: Serves 6 to 8 | Prep Time: 30 minutes | Cook Time: 1 hour

Chicken pot pie always smells so darn good. I think it's the smell of the buttery dough and the combination of vegetables and chicken sautéing. Whatever it is, my husband always migrates away from football and into the kitchen to ask, "How much longer?" Lucky for him, this pot pie casserole is a quick one, but it will taste as if you spent all day making it as magical as it is.

INGREDIENTS

2 (8-ounce) tubes refrigerated original style crescent rolls

1 tablespoon vegetable oil

1 cup diced onion

1 pound boneless, skinless chicken breasts, cooked and cut into ½-inch pieces

2 cups frozen diced potatoes, thawed

12 ounces frozen peas and carrots, thawed

1 cup water

2 (10.75-ounce) cans cream of chicken soup

½ teaspoon poultry seasoning

1 tablespoon whole milk

DIRECTIONS

1. Preheat the oven to 350°F and lightly coat a 9 × 13-inch baking dish with cooking spray.

2. Unroll 1 tube of crescent rolls and place in the baking dish in 1 piece. Use your fingers to press together all the seams and make an even layer of dough in the bottom and partially up the sides of the dish. Bake for 20 minutes.

3. While the bottom crust is baking, heat the oil in a medium skillet over medium-high heat. Add the onion and cook for 2 minutes until translucent, then add the chicken, potatoes, peas and carrots, and the water. Bring to a simmer, cover, and cook for 10 minutes. Uncover and stir in the soup and poultry seasoning. Spoon into the baked crust.

4. Unroll the second tube of crescent rolls and press the seams together to seal, stretching the dough slightly to the size of the baking dish. Lay on top of the filling, sealing the edges. Cut 4 to 6 steam vents into the top crust, brush with the milk, and bake for 25 minutes, until the top crust is browned and cooked through. Serve.

NOTES

To cook the chicken, place the breasts on a baking sheet and bake at 350°F for 30 minutes. Remove from the oven and cut into ½-inch pieces.

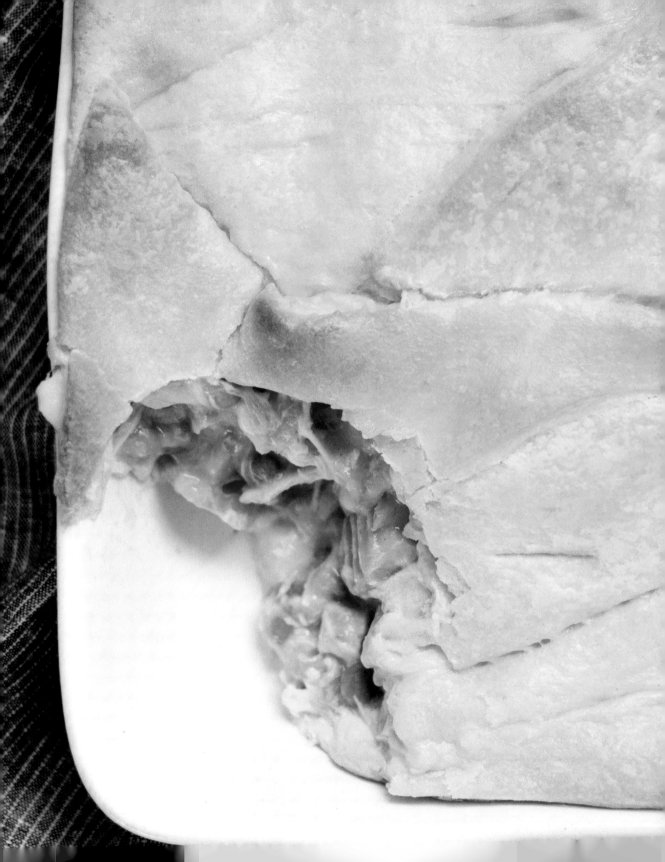

Mom's Chicken Noodle Soup Casserole

Yield: Serves 8 | Prep Time: 20 minutes | Cook Time: 25 minutes

You don't have to be under the weather to enjoy chicken noodle soup. After growing up in Minnesota, where the cold always made it chicken noodle soup weather, I carry on the tradition, despite living elsewhere. This version is not only easy to make, it will bring back warm and fuzzy feelings on a cold or dreary day.

INGREDIENTS

8 ounces wide egg noodles

3 tablespoons unsalted butter

1 small onion, chopped

3 stalks celery, chopped

3 carrots, peeled and chopped

3 garlic cloves, minced

3 tablespoons all-purpose flour

1¼ cups whole milk

2 teaspoons minced fresh thyme, plus more for garnish

1 teaspoon dried basil

1 teaspoon kosher salt

½ teaspoon freshly ground black pepper

2 cups shredded cooked chicken breast meat

1½ cups shredded sharp white cheddar cheese

DIRECTIONS

1. Preheat the oven to 425°F and lightly coat a 9 × 9-inch baking dish with cooking spray.

2. Bring a large pot of water to a boil, add the noodles, cook until al dente, drain, and return to the pot.

3. In a large skillet, melt the butter over medium heat. Add the onion, celery, carrots, and garlic and cook until softened. Whisk the flour into the pan with the vegetables. Add the milk slowly, mixing well to combine, until a sauce is created. Add the thyme, basil, salt, and pepper. Stir in the chicken, noodles, and 1 cup of the cheese.

4. Pour the mixture into the baking dish and top with the remaining cheese. Bake for 10 minutes until warmed through and the cheese has melted on top. Serve, garnished with additional sprigs of thyme.

NOTES

To cook the chicken, place 2 boneless, skinless chicken breasts on a baking sheet and bake at 350°F for 30 minutes. Remove from the oven and shred.

4

Beef and Pork

As a cook, I value how beef yields so many different cuts of meat, which in turn make a huge variety of meals, from hamburgers to steak frites to filet mignon. Similarly, pork gives us bacon in the morning and hot Italian sausage at night. In this chapter you'll find casseroles based on a wide range of beef and pork cuts, from cuisines all over the map.

Scrumptious Sloppy Joe Casserole

Yield: Serves 6 to 8 | Prep Time: 15 minutes | Cook Time: 25 minutes

Sloppy joes are a nostalgic and hearty weeknight meal, and a favorite alternative to a hamburger or chicken sandwich. Combining the zesty ground beef with beans and noodles and baking it all in a casserole dish is a quick way to serve a crowd, or a hungry family.

INGREDIENTS

8 ounces elbow macaroni

2 tablespoons olive oil

1 onion, chopped

1 green bell pepper, chopped

1 pound ground beef

1 (15-ounce) can kidney beans, drained and rinsed

1 (14-ounce) can diced tomatoes

1 (4-ounce) can green chiles

1 cup shredded cheddar cheese

Fresh parsley, for garnish (optional)

DIRECTIONS

1. Preheat the oven to 350°F and lightly coat a 9 × 13-inch baking dish with cooking spray.

2. Bring a large pot of water to a boil, add the macaroni, and cook until al dente. Drain and reserve.

3. In a large skillet, heat the olive oil over medium heat. Add the onion and pepper and sauté until soft. Add the ground beef and cook, stirring to break up the meat, until the meat turns brown and is no longer pink. Drain any remaining grease. Place the skillet back on the heat and add the beans, tomatoes, and chiles. Cook, stirring, for 5 minutes.

4. Combine the tomato-bean mixture with the beef and pour into the baking dish. Top with the cheese and bake for 10 minutes. Serve, garnished with fresh parsley if desired.

Easy Meatball Party Sub Casserole

Yield: Serves 6 to 8 | Prep Time: 15 minutes | Cook Time: 35 minutes

This replicates a typical sub sandwich, but is much easier to make ahead and serve to a group. The bread at the bottom stays crispy while the toppings are hot and bubbly—a perfect party dish to fill up your guests.

INGREDIENTS

2 tablespoons unsalted butter

4 garlic cloves, minced

1 (12-ounce) baguette

8 ounces cream cheese, room temperature

2 tablespoons mayonnaise

½ teaspoon Italian seasoning, plus more for topping

1 pound Italian-style meatballs, thawed if frozen

1 (24-ounce) jar spaghetti sauce

2 cups shredded mozzarella cheese

DIRECTIONS

1. Preheat the oven to broil.

2. Microwave the butter and garlic until the butter melts and brush the bottom of a 9 × 13-inch broiler-safe baking pan with half of the garlic butter.

3. Slice the baguette into 2-inch slices and fit into the baking pan cut side down, cutting some if necessary to fill the bottom of the pan without large gaps. Brush the cut side of all of the bread slices with the remaining butter and garlic. Broil until the top of the bread is golden brown, about 5 minutes. Remove the bread and lower the oven temperature to 350°F.

4. While the bread toasts, combine the cream cheese, mayonnaise, and Italian seasoning in a small bowl and beat until very smooth. Spread this mixture over the toasted bread in an even layer.

5. Cut the meatballs in half and make a layer of them on top of the cheese mixture. Pour the spaghetti sauce over the meatballs and sprinkle with the cheese and additional Italian seasoning. Bake for 30 minutes or until the cheese is melted and the sauce is bubbling hot. Serve.

Reuben Casserole

Yield: Serves 6 to 8 | Prep Time: 20 minutes | Cook Time: 50 minutes

If you like Reuben sandwiches, you'll love this casserole. The sharp, tangy, and sour taste of the rye bread pairs well with the sauerkraut and is complemented by the spicy mustard and rich corned beef. Layered together and baked until bubbling hot, this is a great way to serve a crowd a beloved sandwich.

INGREDIENTS

Russian Dressing

1 cup mayonnaise

¼ cup chili sauce or ketchup

1 tablespoon finely chopped onion, mashed into a paste

1 teaspoon horseradish

1 teaspoon hot sauce

1 teaspoon Worcestershire sauce

¼ teaspoon sweet paprika

¼ teaspoon freshly ground black pepper

⅛ teaspoon salt

Casserole

10–12 slices marbled rye bread, cubed

1 pound sliced deli-style corned beef, roughly chopped

3 tablespoons deli-style mustard

20 ounces sauerkraut, drained and rinsed

1 teaspoon caraway seeds

3 cups shredded Jarlsberg cheese

1 tablespoon unsalted butter, melted

DIRECTIONS

1. Preheat the oven to 350°F and lightly coat a 9 × 13-inch baking dish with cooking spray.

2. For the Russian dressing: Whisk all the dressing ingredients in a medium bowl until combined. Set aside.

3. For the casserole: Layer half of the bread cubes on the bottom of the baking dish. Cover the bread cubes with the corned beef and dot the mustard over the corned beef. Cover the corned beef with the sauerkraut, then sprinkle the caraway seeds over the sauerkraut. Pour ½ cup of the Russian dressing and cover with cheese. (Refrigerate and reserve the remaining Russian dressing for another use.)

4. Layer the remaining bread on top and drizzle the melted butter over the casserole. Bake for 45 to 50 minutes, until the bread is golden and the cheese is melted. Serve.

NOTES

For a faster prep time, you can buy bottled Russian dressing instead of making it from scratch.

John Wayne Cowboy Casserole

Yield: Serves 6 to 8 | Prep Time: 15 minutes | Cook Time: 30 to 35 minutes

When I imagine a pair of cowboy boots propped on a log next to a full pot over an open fire, I imagine that pot filled with biscuits and beans. I have always wanted to hang out at one of those campfires that you see in movies or magazines. I do own three pairs of cowboy boots, so I would do my best to fit in. That said, I am more of a wannabe cowgirl, so I've replicated my vision in a cast-iron skillet and topped the biscuits with tomatillos for a little something extra special.

INGREDIENTS

1 pound ground beef

1 cup chopped onion

2 (16-ounce) cans chili beans, hot or mild

½ cup smoky barbeque sauce

2 cups baking mix

2 tablespoons vegetable oil

2 scallions, finely chopped

⅔ cup whole milk

2 tablespoons grated Parmesan cheese

1 tomatillo, sliced thinly

DIRECTIONS

1. Preheat the oven to 425°F.

2. In a 10-inch cast-iron skillet or other stovetop-to-oven pan, cook the ground beef, stirring to break up the meat, for 5 minutes. Add the onion and continue to cook and stir for an additional 2 minutes. Drain any excess fat and return the meat to the pan. Add the beans and barbeque sauce to the pan and heat just until heated through.

3. Place the baking mix in a medium bowl, stir in 1 tablespoon of the oil and the scallions, then gradually add the milk and stir to form a soft dough. Drop spoonfuls of the dough on top of the beef and bean mixture in the skillet. Brush the tops with the remaining oil and sprinkle with the Parmesan cheese.

4. Bake for 20 to 25 minutes, until the biscuits are cooked through and golden brown on top. Serve, garnished with tomatillo slices.

Beef Noodle Pappardelle Casserole

Yield: Serves 6 to 8 | Prep Time: 45 minutes | Cook Time: 1 hour 20 minutes

If you're picturing tongs pulling out the long noodles, sauce splattering, and family members smiling, you're on the right track. With big buttery noodles, beef, carrots, celery, and seasoned tomato sauce, this casserole will leave smiles on everyone's faces.

INGREDIENTS

3 tablespoons olive oil

1 onion, chopped

4 garlic cloves, minced

1 large carrot, peeled and coarsely chopped

1 large stalk celery, coarsely chopped

1 pound ground beef

1 (28-ounce) can crushed tomatoes

¼ cup chopped parsley

2 tablespoons tomato paste

½ teaspoon kosher salt

½ teaspoon freshly ground black pepper

2 pinches sugar

12 ounces pappardelle

¼ cup heavy cream

¼ cup grated Pecorino Romano cheese

1 cup shredded mozzarella cheese

DIRECTIONS

1. Preheat the oven to 375°F and lightly coat a 9 × 13-inch baking dish with cooking spray.

2. In a large skillet, heat the olive oil over medium heat and sauté the onion and garlic for 7 to 8 minutes. Add the carrot and celery and cook for 5 minutes. Add the ground beef and cook, stirring to break up the meat, until no longer pink. Add the tomatoes, parsley, tomato paste, salt, pepper, and sugar. Cook for 30 minutes.

3. While the sauce is cooking, bring a large pot of water to a boil, add the pappardelle, and cook until al dente. Drain, and reserve.

4. Add the cream and then the Pecorino Romano to the sauce. Toss the sauce with the cooked pasta and place in the baking dish. Top with the mozzarella and bake for 30 minutes. Serve.

Scalloped Potato and Beef Casserole

Yield: Serves 6 to 8 | Prep Time: 30 minutes | Cook Time: 1 hour 40 minutes

Who said gravy was the only thing to top potatoes with? Try sautéed beef and golden mushrooms to break out of your dinner routine. The smell of rosemary will fill the kitchen, making this a meal to eat by the fire, curled up at home.

INGREDIENTS

1½ pounds lean ground beef

1 (8-ounce) package cremini mushrooms, sliced

1 onion, chopped

1 red bell pepper, chopped

5 garlic cloves, minced

½ teaspoon crushed red pepper flakes

2 (10.75-ounce) cans cream of mushroom soup

¾ cup heavy cream

½ cup sour cream

⅓ cup minced shallots

¼ cup grated Parmesan cheese

2 teaspoons minced fresh rosemary, plus additional sprigs for garnish

½ teaspoon kosher salt

Freshly ground black pepper

6 russet potatoes, peeled and very thinly sliced

1 cup shredded cheddar cheese

1 cup shredded Gruyère cheese

DIRECTIONS

1. Preheat the oven to 350°F and lightly coat a 9 × 13-inch baking dish with cooking spray.

2. In a large skillet over medium heat, cook the ground beef with the mushrooms, onion, bell pepper, 4 cloves of the garlic, and the pepper flakes, stirring to break up the meat, until the beef is no longer pink. In a bowl, combine the soup, cream, sour cream, shallots, Parmesan, rosemary, remaining garlic, salt, and pepper to taste.

3. Layer the sliced potatoes in the bottom of the baking dish and top with the soup mixture. Sprinkle half of the cheddar and half of the Gruyère over the soup mixture and top with the meat mixture. Cover with foil and bake for 1 hour.

4. Remove the foil and bake for an additional 30 minutes, until the potatoes are tender. Remove from the oven, top with the remaining cheddar and Gruyère, and bake for 5 minutes until the cheese has melted. Serve, garnished with fresh rosemary.

Classic Shepherd's Pie Casserole

Yield: Serves 6 | Prep Time: 30 minutes | Cook Time: 40 minutes

Shepherd's pie, also known as cottage pie, is made out of meat and vegetables and topped with a layer of golden mashed potatoes. When you think of it, it makes perfect sense: a savory twist on the original apple. Ground beef makes for a hearty filling and the potatoes replace that flaky, sweet crust. This good ol' meat-and-potatoes dish will go down easy.

INGREDIENTS

1 teaspoon olive oil

1 onion, chopped

2 pounds ground sirloin

2 cups frozen mixed vegetables

3 tablespoons tomato paste

½ teaspoon salt

½ teaspoon freshly ground black pepper

2 cups beef broth

2 tablespoons all-purpose flour

1 (20-ounce) package refrigerated mashed potatoes, or homemade

Fresh sage for garnish (optional)

DIRECTIONS

1. Preheat the oven to 375°F and lightly coat a 7 × 11-inch baking dish with cooking spray.

2. In a 12-inch skillet, heat the olive oil over medium-high heat. Add the onion and cook for 5 minutes, stirring occasionally, until soft. Add the sirloin and cook for 5 to 7 minutes, stirring occasionally, until thoroughly cooked. Drain any excess fat and return the meat to the pan.

3. Add the mixed vegetables, tomato paste, salt, and pepper; cook over medium heat for 5 minutes, stirring frequently, until the vegetables are hot. In a small bowl, whisk the broth and flour together. Add the broth mixture to the beef mixture. Heat to boiling; cook for 3 minutes, stirring constantly, until thick.

4. Spoon the beef mixture into the baking dish. Spread the mashed potatoes over the beef mixture; fluff with a fork. Bake for 20 minutes, until the potatoes are golden brown. Serve, garnished with fresh sage leaves if desired.

Philly Cheesesteak Casserole

Yield: Serves 6 to 8 | Prep Time: 20 minutes | Cook Time: 40 minutes

While Philadelphians debate where to find the best cheesesteak in their city, I am popping my casserole version of the legendary sandwich in the oven! With thinly sliced steak, peppers, and cheese folded into a toasted hoagie, this casserole is a fun way to replicate the original.

INGREDIENTS

2 tablespoons olive oil

1 onion, diced

1 green bell pepper, sliced

1 red bell pepper, sliced

1 orange bell pepper, sliced

4 garlic cloves, minced

1½ pounds beef steak, thinly sliced

1 cup red wine

½ cup ketchup

¼ cup soy sauce

2 tablespoons Worcestershire sauce

1 tablespoon Sriracha

1 tablespoon ground ginger

2 cups provolone cheese, sliced

Hoagie rolls, for serving

DIRECTIONS

1. Preheat the oven to 400°F and lightly coat a 9 × 13-inch baking dish with cooking spray.

2. In a large saucepan heat the olive oil over medium heat. Add the onion, bell peppers, and garlic, and sauté until soft, about 5 minutes.

3. Add beef steak and stir, breaking up and browning. Cook until the beef turns brown. Drain any remaining grease.

4. Add the wine, ketchup, soy sauce, Worcestershire sauce, Sriracha, and ginger to the saucepan and stir to combine. Simmer for 5 minutes.

5. Pour the mixture into the baking dish and top with the cheese.

6. Bake for 20 minutes, until the cheese is bubbling. Serve hot with the hoagie rolls.

Six-Ingredient Stuffed Peppers

Yield: Serves 6 | Prep Time: 20 minutes | Cook Time: 1 hour

When I throw a party, I like to have munchies (things in bowls set around the house), grab-and-holds (like cheese and crackers), and sit-downs (foods you can sit with and enjoy if you are a little hungrier). This recipe is a great sit-down appetizer for a dinner party, and can stand alone as a weeknight dinner. Stuffed with just a few ingredients, including ground beef and seasoned rice, these individually served peppers are one of my favorite foods.

INGREDIENTS

1 (6.9-ounce) box rice pilaf mix with seasoning packet

1 onion, chopped

4 garlic cloves, minced

1½ pounds lean ground beef

6 large bell peppers, red or green or both

Salt and freshly ground black pepper

1 cup tomato juice

Fresh cilantro for garnish (optional)

DIRECTIONS

1. Preheat the oven to 350°F and lightly coat an 8 × 8-inch baking dish with cooking spray.

2. Cook the rice according to the package directions, using the spice packet included in the box.

3. Meanwhile, in a large skillet, sauté the onion and garlic over medium-high heat for 3 minutes. Add the beef and cook, stirring to break up the meat, for 5 to 7 minutes, until no longer pink.

4. Cut the peppers in half lengthwise and remove the stems, seeds, and ribs inside.

5. When the rice is cooked, fluff with a fork and add to the beef. Season with salt and pepper to taste.

6. Arrange 6 pepper halves on the bottom of the baking dish, skin side down. Spoon the rice-beef mixture into the dish and pour the tomato juice over the top. Top with the remaining pepper halves (like a turtle shell covering the filled pepper). Cover the dish with foil and bake for 45 minutes. Remove the foil and check to see if the peppers are soft; if not, return to the oven, uncovered, and cook for another 5 to 10 minutes. Serve, garnished with fresh cilantro if desired.

Minnesota Hot Dish

Yield: Serves 4 | Prep Time: 15 minutes | Cook Time: 50 minutes

My family runs a corn and cattle farm in Minnesota, so you could say this dish is right up my alley, as I am a meat-and-potatoes kind of gal. I remember running into the farmhouse upon hearing the big brass dinner bell ring, and although we don't have a bell in our home, the dinging of the timer or closing of the oven door acts as a similar cue. When this dish is served, it's not hard to call people into the kitchen.

INGREDIENTS

1 onion, diced

2 tablespoons olive oil

1 pound ground beef

1 (16-ounce) package frozen mixed vegetables

1 (10.75-ounce) can cream of mushroom soup

½ cup whole milk

1 cup shredded cheddar cheese

½ teaspoon salt

1 (32-ounce) package frozen potato puffs

DIRECTIONS

1. Preheat the oven to 400°F and lightly coat an 8 × 8-inch baking dish with cooking spray.

2. In a large skillet, sauté the onion in olive oil over medium heat. Add the ground beef and cook, stirring to break up the meat, until the meat is no longer pink. Drain any excess fat and return the meat to the pan. Add the frozen vegetables, soup, milk, cheese, and salt. Stir and simmer for 2 minutes.

3. Pour into the baking dish and top with the frozen potato puffs. Bake for 40 minutes, until the potatoes are golden and heated through. Serve.

Taco Crescent Casserole

Yield: Serves 6 | Prep Time: 15 minutes | Cook Time: 35 minutes

Taco night just got easier! Combine your ingredients, top with a crescent lid, and bake until you're ready to serve. This recipe is such a fun twist on the taco, and combining it all in one dish makes for easy, contained cleanup.

INGREDIENTS

1 pound ground beef

1 onion, diced

2 tablespoons taco seasoning

1 (11-ounce) can Mexican blend corn

1 (5.5-ounce) can tomato juice

2 (8-ounce) tubes refrigerated original style crescent rolls

1 cup shredded Monterey Jack cheese

DIRECTIONS

1. Preheat the oven to 375°F and lightly coat a 9-inch pie plate with cooking spray.

2. In a large skillet, cook the ground beef over medium-high heat, stirring to break up the meat, until no longer pink, about 5 minutes. Add the onion and seasoning mix and continue to cook, stirring, for 2 minutes. Add the corn and tomato juice and simmer for 2 minutes.

3. Unroll 1 tube of crescent rolls and separate into triangles. Arrange them in the pie plate and stretch and press with your fingers to make a crust without any holes.

4. Spoon the filling into the crust and top with the cheese. Unroll and separate the second tube of rolls. Arrange the triangles on top with the points in the center, leaving space between each triangle. Press the edges to seal, then crimp with the tines of a fork. Bake for 25 minutes, until the crust is completely cooked and golden brown. Serve.

Loaded Pulled Pork and Potato Casserole

Yield: Serves 8 | Prep Time: 1 hour | Cook Time: 55 minutes

Top creamy mashed potatoes with pulled pork and you've got yourself a party in a pot. But unlike most pulled pork recipes, this one doesn't require hours of slow cooking. Store-bought, aka semi-homemade, is sometimes the best way to go, and this casserole is proof.

INGREDIENTS

4 pounds store-bought precooked barbeque pork

3 pounds Yukon Gold potatoes, peeled and cut

6 ounces cream cheese

½ cup sour cream

½ cup half-and-half

4 tablespoons unsalted butter

½ teaspoon kosher salt

½ teaspoon freshly ground black pepper

8 ounces bacon, cooked and crumbled

4 scallions, thinly sliced

12 ounces shredded sharp cheddar cheese

1 small jalapeño pepper, seeds removed, minced

Fresh rosemary for garnish (optional)

DIRECTIONS

1. Preheat the oven to 400°F and lightly coat a 9 × 13-inch baking dish with cooking spray.

2. Heat the barbeque pork according to the directions on the package. Bring a large pot of salted water to a boil, add the potatoes, and cook until tender, about 45 minutes.

3. Drain the potatoes and mash them with the cream cheese, sour cream, half-and-half, butter, salt, and pepper. Add the bacon, scallions, and half of the cheese.

4. Place the potato mixture in the baking dish. Top with the heated barbeque pork, the remaining cheese, and the jalapeño.

5. Place in the oven and heat until the cheese has melted, 5 to 10 minutes. Serve, garnished with fresh rosemary if desired.

5

Vegetarian

You don't have to be a full-time vegetarian to enjoy a meatless meal or two! These dishes are all packed with flavor, good-for-you vegetables, and grains that will fill you up any day of the week.

Veggie Medley Casserole

Yield: Serves 4 to 6 | Prep Time: 10 minutes | Cook Time: 35 minutes

Picky-eater troubles? Say no more. An assortment of good-for-you vegetables, mixed with cream and cheddar cheeses and baked until warm and gooey, will have even the most skeptical veggie haters coming back for seconds!

INGREDIENTS

1 (3-pound) bag frozen mixed vegetables (cauliflower, broccoli, carrots), thawed

4 tablespoons unsalted butter

2 tablespoons all-purpose flour

1 teaspoon minced onion

1 cup whole milk

½ teaspoon salt

½ teaspoon freshly ground black pepper

4 ounces cream cheese

1 cup shredded cheddar cheese

DIRECTIONS

1. Preheat the oven to 350°F.

2. Microwave the mixed vegetables until heated through, according to package instructions, and pour into an 8 × 8-inch baking dish.

3. In a large saucepan, whisk the butter, flour, and onion over medium heat for 3 minutes. Add the milk, salt, and pepper, then add the cream cheese and stir until smooth. Pour the cream cheese sauce over the vegetables. Sprinkle with the cheese and bake for 30 minutes. Serve.

Everyday Eggplant Parmesan

Yield: Serves 6 | Prep Time: 20 minutes | Cook Time: 50 minutes

Eggplant Parmesan is usually breaded, hot, and gooey. This version is too, but combined with fresh tomatoes and peppers, it makes for an ideal summer meal chock-full of colorful fresh ingredients. Thinly sliced and stacked, this casserole is a beautiful dish to serve al fresco, on a patio or deck with a cold glass of white wine.

INGREDIENTS

2 eggplants, each about 8 inches long

2 teaspoons kosher salt

½ cup olive oil

2 large onions, thinly sliced

2 garlic cloves, thinly sliced

4 large ripe tomatoes, sliced ¼ inch thick

8 ounces mozzarella cheese, sliced

2 large bell peppers, red or green or both, sliced ¼ inch thick

Freshly ground black pepper

1 cup tomato sauce

½ cup grated Parmesan cheese

¼ cup thinly sliced fresh basil

¼ cup chopped parsley

DIRECTIONS

1. Preheat the oven to 375°F and lightly coat an 8 × 8-inch baking dish with cooking spray.

2. Slice the eggplants ¼ inch thick. Arrange them in a large colander set over a large bowl and sprinkle liberally with the salt; let stand for 15 to 20 minutes.

3. In a large, heavy skillet, heat the olive oil over medium-high heat. Add the onions and garlic and sauté until softened but not browned, about 10 minutes.

4. Lay the eggplant slices on a paper towel–lined baking sheet and pat dry. Brush both sides of each slice with some of the flavored oil in the skillet.

5. Starting at one end of the casserole dish, begin layering the eggplant, tomatoes, mozzarella, and bell pepper, alternating each item until you reach the other end of the casserole.

6. Grind some black pepper over the dish, then scatter the onions and garlic over the top. Add the tomato sauce and Parmesan, and cover the dish with foil.

7. Bake for 40 minutes, until the eggplant is soft and the casserole is bubbling. Add the parsley and basil on top and serve.

NOTES

Salting the eggplant brings moisture to its surface and removes any slightly bitter flavor.

Low-Carb Zesty Zucchini Casserole

Yield: Serves 4 | Prep Time: 20 minutes | Cook Time: 35 minutes

Sweet corn combined with superthin zucchini and zested up with spice makes for a delightful low-carb pasta alternative. Baked in Parmesan and cream, it's a light but satisfying side to eat along with a salad, steak, or salmon.

INGREDIENTS

2 tablespoons olive oil

4 zucchini, thinly sliced

1 (15.25-ounce) can whole kernel corn, drained

1 leek, thinly sliced

1 teaspoon salt

1 teaspoon freshly ground black pepper

½ teaspoon garlic powder

1 cup grated Parmesan cheese

½ cup half-and-half

3 bay leaves

DIRECTIONS

1. Preheat the oven to 375°F and lightly coat an 8 × 8-inch baking dish with cooking spray.

2. In a large skillet, heat the olive oil over medium heat; add the zucchini and sauté, flipping occasionally, for about 5 minutes. Add the corn, leek, salt, pepper, and garlic powder.

3. Remove from the heat, add the cheese, half-and-half, and bay leaves, and pour into the baking dish. Bake for 30 minutes, until hot and bubbling. Remove the bay leaves. Serve.

Vegetarian Southwestern Casserole

Yield: Serves 6 | Prep Time: 20 minutes | Cook Time: 30 minutes

What I love about this cheesy Southwestern-inspired enchilada casserole is that it is not only good for you, but also vegetarian. Packed with fiber from beans and whole wheat, this will fill you up with plenty of vegetables.

INGREDIENTS

6 (8-inch) whole-wheat tortillas

2 teaspoons olive oil

1 cup chopped onion

1 cup chopped red bell pepper

1 tablespoon minced garlic

1 (15-ounce) can black beans, drained and rinsed

1 (11-ounce) can Mexican-style corn, drained

1 (4.5-ounce) can chopped green chiles

¼ cup chopped fresh cilantro, plus extra for serving

1 teaspoon chili powder

½ teaspoon ground cumin

½ teaspoon salt

¼ teaspoon freshly ground black pepper

1 (16-ounce) can fat-free refried beans

1 (10-ounce) can enchilada sauce, mild or hot

1 cup shredded Mexican cheese blend

Light sour cream

DIRECTIONS

1. Preheat the oven to 375°F. Line a baking sheet with foil and spray with cooking spray. Lightly coat a 9 × 13-inch baking dish with cooking spray.

2. Cut the tortillas into quarters and lay on the baking sheet; spray with cooking spray and place in the oven as it preheats, until the tortillas begin to crisp and brown, about 5 minutes.

3. In a large skillet, heat the olive oil over medium-high heat. Add the onion, bell pepper, and garlic, and cook until the vegetables soften, about 2 minutes. Add the beans, corn, chiles, cilantro, chili powder, cumin, salt, and pepper and cook, stirring, just until warmed through.

4. Place the crisped tortillas in the bottom of the baking dish and spread the refried beans evenly on top. Add the sautéed vegetable and black bean mixture in an even layer and top with the enchilada sauce. Sprinkle the cheese over the casserole and bake for 20 minutes, until hot and bubbling and the cheese is melted. Garnish with cilantro and sour cream and serve.

Quinoa and Pepper Medley Casserole

Yield: Serves 6 to 8 | Prep Time: 20 minutes | Cook Time: 55 minutes

Did you know that quinoa is a superfood? Packed with fiber, minerals, and protein, quinoa offers a lot of nutritional bang for the buck. Add beans and this dish will give you enough energy and good-for-you nutrients to power through your evening to-dos.

INGREDIENTS

¾ cup quinoa, rinsed and drained

1½ cups water

5 teaspoons vegetable oil

1 cup chopped onion

1 red bell pepper, sliced

1 green bell pepper, sliced

1 poblano pepper, sliced

¼ cup finely diced jalapeño peppers

1 tablespoon finely minced garlic

1 teaspoon chili powder

1 teaspoon ground cumin

1 teaspoon salt

½ teaspoon cayenne pepper

2 (15-ounce) cans black beans, drained and rinsed

1½ cups shredded Mexican cheese blend

DIRECTIONS

1. Preheat the oven to 375°F and lightly coat a 9 × 9-inch baking dish with cooking spray.

2. In a medium cooking pot, cook the quinoa in 1½ cups of water over medium heat for 15 minutes, until tender and most of the liquid has been absorbed.

3. In a large skillet, heat 1 tablespoon of the oil over medium-high heat. Add the onion, bell peppers, poblano, jalapeños, and garlic and sauté for 6 to 8 minutes. Transfer the pepper mixture to a bowl.

4. Add the quinoa, chili powder, cumin, salt, and cayenne pepper to the empty skillet and cook, stirring, over medium-high heat until the quinoa is toasted and fragrant, about 2 minutes.

5. Place the beans in the baking dish. Spoon the quinoa over the beans in a smooth layer, scatter the peppers on top, and then add the cheese. Cover with foil and bake for 20 minutes, then remove the foil and bake for an additional 10 minutes, until bubbling and the cheese is melted. Serve.

Summer Veggie Casserole

Yield: Serves 6 | Prep Time: 30 minutes | Cook Time: 1 hour

Freshly prepared seasonal produce is one of my favorite things to serve in the summer, when I'm in the mood for something cooked, yet still fresh and light. In the months of salads, sandwiches, and cold ice cream treats, this warm burst of color is a welcome addition to potlucks and picnics!

INGREDIENTS

6 large Swiss chard leaves and stems

1 tablespoon olive oil

1 large leek, sliced

3 scallions, sliced

½ cup vegetable broth

½ cup plain Greek yogurt

2 tablespoons all-purpose flour

1 teaspoon minced fresh oregano or ½ teaspoon dried oregano, plus extra for serving

2 yellow summer squash, thinly sliced

2 zucchini, thinly sliced

2 tomatoes, thinly sliced

½ teaspoon salt

¼ teaspoon freshly ground black pepper

⅓ cup Italian-style bread crumbs

2 tablespoons grated Parmesan cheese

2 teaspoons unsalted butter, melted

DIRECTIONS

1. Preheat the oven to 375°F and lightly coat a 9-inch deep-dish pie plate with cooking spray.

2. Remove the Swiss chard stems from the leaves and chop the stems and leaves separately. In a medium skillet, heat the olive oil over medium-high heat, add the leek, scallions, and chard leaves, and sauté, stirring frequently, for about 3 minutes. Add the chard stems, cover, and continue to cook for another 5 minutes, until very soft.

3. Meanwhile stir the broth, yogurt, flour, and oregano together in a small bowl until smooth. Add to the chard mixture and cook, stirring, about 1 minute.

4. Layer half the yellow squash, zucchini, tomatoes, and chard mixture into the baking dish and sprinkle with a pinch of the salt and pepper. Repeat with the remaining vegetables and sprinkle with more salt and pepper.

5. Combine the bread crumbs, cheese, and melted butter in a small bowl and sprinkle on top of the vegetables. Cover the casserole with foil and bake for 40 minutes, then remove the foil and bake for an additional 10 minutes, until the crumbs are browned. Sprinkle with oregano and serve.

Grilled Cheese and Tomato Soup Casserole

Yield: Serves 6 to 8 | Prep Time: 30 minutes | Cook Time: 35 minutes

I remember thinking as a kid whenever someone made a grilled cheese sandwich that they must be a professional cook. I think it was the flipping of the bread and perfect browning that made this sandwich seem more like a culinary feat than the peanut butter and jelly I was used to. When served with tomato soup, this simple meal felt so fancy. During my years working in culinary design, mashing up two beloved foods into one was a trend I saw often and loved. Grilled cheese and tomato soup are an ideal pair for this mash-up. Combining that rich and creamy tomato soup texture and taste with toasted bread and cheese, this ultimate comfort food is even better in casserole form.

INGREDIENTS

3 ounces cream cheese, softened

12 (½-inch-thick) slices Italian or sourdough bread, lightly toasted

6 fresh basil leaves, thinly sliced

6 slices provolone cheese

4 tablespoons unsalted butter

½ cup tomato sauce

1 garlic clove, minced

¼ teaspoon salt

¼ teaspoon freshly ground black pepper

1¾ cups half-and-half

2 large eggs

1 cup shredded Italian cheese blend

DIRECTIONS

1. Preheat the oven to 350°F and lightly coat a 9 × 13-inch baking dish with cooking spray.

2. Spread the cream cheese onto 6 slices of bread and sprinkle the basil over the cream cheese. Top with the provolone and the remaining bread slices and butter the top of each sandwich. Place the sandwiches in the baking dish.

3. In a medium saucepan, combine the tomato sauce, garlic, salt, and pepper over medium heat. Cook for 1 minute. Slowly whisk in the half-and-half and bring to a boil. Reduce the heat and simmer for 4 to 5 minutes, until a thick sauce forms.

4. Whisk the eggs in a large bowl. Slowly add one-third of the tomato mixture. Whisk for 2 to 3 minutes.

5. Add the remaining tomato mixture. Pour over the sandwiches and sprinkle the Italian cheese blend over the top.

6. Bake for 25 to 30 minutes, until golden and the cheese has melted. Serve.

Best Baked Ravioli

Yield: Serves 6 to 8 | Prep Time: 20 minutes | Cook Time: 45 minutes

Say good-bye to watery, soggy ravioli and hello to crispy, golden, cheesy goodness. The ravioli crisp up in the oven, and they sit perfectly in the rich, buttery tomatoes. Once spooned onto plates, the thick cheesy sauce holds its own with these crispy little pillows of cheese.

INGREDIENTS

2 pounds cheese ravioli, unthawed if frozen

2 tablespoons olive oil

1 cup chopped onion

1 tablespoon minced garlic

½ teaspoon crushed red pepper flakes

3 tablespoons chopped fresh basil leaves

1 (28-ounce) can tomato puree

1 (14-ounce) can diced tomatoes

1 cup shredded mozzarella cheese

½ cup grated Parmesan cheese

DIRECTIONS

1. Preheat the oven to 400°F and lightly coat a 9 × 13-inch baking dish with cooking spray.

2. Bring a large pot of water to boil, add 1 teaspoon salt and ravioli and cook until al dente. Drain and toss with 1 tablespoon of the olive oil.

3. In a medium skillet, heat the remaining 1 tablespoon oil over medium-high heat, add the onion, and sauté for 3 minutes, until the onion is translucent. Add the garlic, pepper flakes, and basil and cook until fragrant, about 1 minute. Add the tomato puree and diced tomatoes and lower the heat to a simmer. Cook for 10 minutes, stirring frequently.

4. Combine the sauce and ravioli, stirring gently so the ravioli stay intact. Place in the baking dish and sprinkle the mozzarella, then the Parmesan, over the top. Bake for 15 to 20 minutes, until hot and bubbling. Serve.

Caprese Quinoa Casserole

Yield: Serves 8 | Prep Time: 30 minutes | Cook Time: 45 minutes

We've all enjoyed a traditional caprese salad with layered mozzarella and tomatoes, a hint of basil, and balsamic vinaigrette. You may think there is no improving on perfection, but this is a slightly new take, a hot one, in casserole form, and believe me when I tell you there is a time and place for both the traditional and this twist! Not only is this dish absolutely stunning, but it is also packed with essential amino acids. Light, refreshing, and good for you, it's the perfect side (or main) dish on a hot summer day when heirloom tomatoes are in season.

INGREDIENTS

2 cups quinoa, rinsed and drained

2 tablespoons extra-virgin olive oil

2 small shallots, minced

3 garlic cloves, minced

2 cups cherry tomatoes, halved

8 ounces fresh part-skim mozzarella cheese, shredded

Kosher salt

Freshly ground black pepper

3 heirloom tomatoes, sliced into ¼-inch-thick rounds

8 ounces fresh part-skim mozzarella cheese, sliced into ¼-inch rounds

¼ cup packed basil leaves, thinly sliced

¼ cup balsamic vinegar

DIRECTIONS

1. Preheat the oven to 400°F and lightly coat a 9-inch pie plate with cooking spray.

2. In a large pot, cook the quinoa in 4 cups of water over medium heat for 15 minutes, until tender.

3. In a medium skillet, heat the olive oil over medium heat. Add the shallots and garlic and sauté for 2 minutes. Add the cherry tomatoes and cook for 2 to 4 minutes while stirring.

4. In a large bowl, combine the quinoa with the sautéed tomato mixture. Stir in the shredded mozzarella, salt, and pepper and transfer to the pie plate.

5. Starting in the center and overlapping them slightly, arrange the tomato and mozzarella slices in a small spiral over the filling.

6. Bake for 30 minutes. Sprinkle the basil over the top, drizzle with the balsamic vinegar, and serve.

Pumpkin Ricotta Pasta Casserole

Yield: Serves 6 to 8 | Prep Time: 20 minutes | Cook Time: 40 minutes

Combine pumpkin, ricotta, and thick tubes of pasta and the result is a vegetarian side dish or main meal for any cold-weather occasion. I served this last year at Thanksgiving with leftover pumpkin from pie making, and not a single guest left without the recipe!

INGREDIENTS

1 pound rigatoni

1 (15-ounce) container ricotta cheese

1 (15-ounce) can pumpkin puree

3 large eggs

½ cup Greek yogurt

2 teaspoons salt

1 teaspoon freshly ground black pepper

½ teaspoon ground nutmeg

1 cup grated Parmesan cheese

1 cup pecans, chopped

4 sage leaves

DIRECTIONS

1. Preheat the oven to 375°F and lightly coat a 9 × 13-inch baking dish with cooking spray.

2. Bring a large pot of water to a boil, add the rigatoni, and cook until al dente. Drain and return the rigatoni to the pot.

3. While the rigatoni is cooking, combine the ricotta, pumpkin, eggs, and yogurt in a large bowl. Add the salt, pepper, and nutmeg. Pour the sauce over the pasta and coat completely.

4. Pour into the baking dish and top with the Parmesan cheese and pecans. Bake for 30 minutes. Top with the sage leaves and serve.

6

Healthy

"Healthy" doesn't mean tasteless or boring, and the following dishes will prove it! From meatballs to tuna salad, cheeseburger casserole (that's right—a skinny version of a favorite indulgence), and creamy coconut chicken, these recipes ensure that you won't be missing out when trying to lighten your meals.

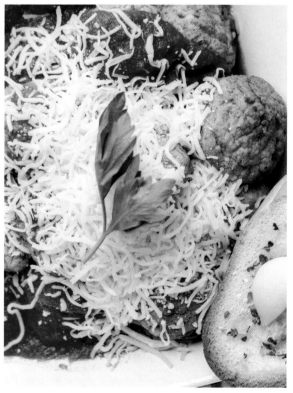

Turkey Meatball Casserole

Yield: Serves 6 | Prep Time: 20 minutes | Cook Time: 1 hour

Food doesn't have to *taste* healthy to be healthy, but it always makes me smile when my husband says, "I can tell it's healthy." I am not sure what that means exactly. The other night when I made this casserole, I didn't hear that age-old comment. He didn't think it was a healthy meal, because the healthy ingredients come together in a way that makes you think you're eating rich and indulgent meatballs—a win-win.

INGREDIENTS

1 pound ground turkey

1 cup plus 3 tablespoons grated Parmesan cheese

½ cup panko bread crumbs

1 large egg

1 tablespoon Italian seasoning

2 garlic cloves, minced

½ teaspoon kosher salt

¼ teaspoon freshly ground black pepper

1 (24-ounce) jar marinara sauce

1½ cups shredded Italian cheese blend

Fresh parsley for garnish (optional)

DIRECTIONS

1. Preheat the oven to 350°F and spray a foil-lined baking sheet with cooking spray. Lightly coat a 9 × 13-inch baking dish with cooking spray.

2. Mix together the ground turkey, 3 tablespoons of the Parmesan, the panko, egg, Italian seasoning, garlic, salt, and pepper until combined. Roll or scoop into 1½-inch balls.

3. Place the meatballs on the baking sheet and bake for 25 to 30 minutes until browned.

4. Pour half of the marinara sauce into the baking dish. Top the sauce with the meatballs, pour the remaining sauce on top, and cover with the remaining Parmesan and the Italian cheese blend. Cover with foil and bake for 30 minutes. Remove the foil and bake an additional 5 minutes until the cheese is browned and bubbling. Serve, garnished with fresh parsley if desired.

Tuna Salad Casserole

Yield: Serves 4 | Prep Time: 15 minutes | Cook Time: 30 minutes

Tiny shells, coated in light cheese and tossed with celery and carrots, might remind you of cold tuna pasta salad, but this version is baked until golden and delicious. Eat this dish warm or cold. It's good either way, and full of lean protein from the tuna.

INGREDIENTS

1 tablespoon olive oil

1½ pounds medium pasta shells

2 tablespoons unsalted butter

2 tablespoons all-purpose flour

1 cup heavy cream

2 tablespoons light mayonnaise

1 teaspoon salt

¾ teaspoon freshly ground black pepper

2 (5-ounce) cans albacore tuna, drained

2 carrots, diced

4 celery stalks, diced

1 cup crushed butter crackers

DIRECTIONS

1. Preheat the oven to 375°F and lightly coat an 8 × 8-inch baking dish with cooking spray.

2. Bring a large pot of water to a boil, add the olive oil and pasta, and cook until al dente. Drain and return to the pot.

3. In a medium saucepan, melt the butter over medium heat, add the flour, and stir. Add the cream, mayonnaise, salt, and pepper and stir to combine. Add the tuna, carrots, and celery.

4. Pour the sauce over the pasta and stir to coat. Pour into the baking dish, top with the crushed crackers, and bake for 15 minutes. Serve.

Skinny Broccoli, Cauliflower, and Ham Casserole

Yield: Serves 6 | Prep Time: 20 minutes | Cook Time: 1 hour

I know this doesn't necessarily scream "healthy" when you look at it, but it is! The sauce that looks like cheese is actually pureed broccoli with milk and reduced-fat cheese, so it's plenty creamy without the cream. A great side dish or main meal, this is chock-full of veggies, protein, and flavor.

INGREDIENTS

1 tablespoon olive oil

2 cups sliced onions

1 pound broccoli florets

2 pounds cauliflower florets

1 cup shredded reduced-fat cheddar cheese

¾ cup skim milk

½ teaspoon salt

¼ teaspoon freshly ground black pepper

1 (7-ounce) ham steak, cut into ½-inch dice

Fresh parsley, chopped, for garnish

DIRECTIONS

1. Preheat the oven to 400°F and lightly coat a 9 × 13-inch baking dish with cooking spray.

2. In a medium skillet, heat the olive oil over medium heat. Add the onions and stir to coat with the oil, then turn the heat to low and cook with minimal stirring for 20 to 25 minutes, until the onions are caramelized.

3. While the onions cook, bring a large pot of salted water to a boil and cook the broccoli until done, approximately 5 minutes. Drain and reserve. Refill the pot with water and repeat with the cauliflower.

4. In a food processor, combine half of the cooked broccoli with half of the cheese, the milk, salt, and pepper and puree to a smooth sauce.

5. Place the remaining broccoli and the cauliflower in the baking dish and add the ham. Sprinkle the remaining cheese over the ham and top with the caramelized onions.

6. Pour the sauce over the casserole and bake for 25 to 30 minutes, until the sauce is warm. Serve, garnished with fresh parsley.

Coconut Chicken and Rice Casserole

Yield: Serves 6 to 8 | Prep Time: 20 minutes | Cook Time: 45 minutes

Coconut milk, red bell pepper, thin rice, and chicken all come together for a light and vibrant result. Velvety with coconut milk, a dairy-free alternative to cow's milk, and vitamin-rich zucchini, this casserole only takes 20 minutes to assemble, so you'll have plenty of time to whip up a mojito or piña colada before dinner is ready!

INGREDIENTS

2 tablespoons olive oil

2 zucchini, sliced

1 (15.25-ounce) can whole kernel corn, drained

1 leek, sliced

1 red bell pepper, sliced

1 (6.3-ounce) box rice pilaf, cooked according to the package directions

5 boneless, skinless chicken breasts, cooked and shredded

1 (13-ounce) can coconut milk

1 teaspoon freshly ground black pepper

DIRECTIONS

1. Preheat the oven to 350°F and lightly coat a 9 × 13-inch baking dish with cooking spray.

2. In a large skillet, heat the olive oil over medium heat. Add the zucchini, corn, leek, and bell pepper, and sauté for 6 to 8 minutes.

3. Combine the vegetables, cooked rice, chicken, coconut milk, and pepper and pour into the baking dish. Bake for 35 minutes, until the coconut milk is absorbed. Serve.

NOTES

To cook the chicken, place the breasts on a baking sheet and bake at 350°F for 30 minutes. Remove from the oven, let cool, and shred.

Skinny Cheeseburger Casserole

Yield: Serves 6 to 8 | Prep Time: 20 minutes | Cook Time: 30 minutes

"Skinny" and "cheeseburger" rarely come together in the same sentence, but when they do, it's a pretty darn good thing. Whole-wheat pasta, rich in fiber, replaces the traditional bun, and adding light cheese and tomatoes instead of ketchup keeps this lower in fat and sugar. Don't be afraid to clean your plate and ask for seconds.

INGREDIENTS

8 ounces whole-wheat elbow macaroni or penne

2 teaspoons olive oil

½ cup finely chopped onion

1 tablespoon finely minced garlic

1 pound ground turkey

1 teaspoon steak seasoning

2 (14.5-ounce) cans diced tomatoes

2 tablespoons tomato paste

1 tablespoon yellow mustard

1 tablespoon dill pickle relish

6 slices (6 ounces) reduced-fat cheddar cheese

Diced tomatoes

Salt and freshly ground black pepper

DIRECTIONS

1. Preheat the oven to 350°F.

2. Bring a large pot of salted water to a boil, add the pasta, and cook until al dente. Drain and reserve.

3. Meanwhile, in a 12-inch ovenproof skillet, heat the olive oil over medium-high heat. Add the onion and garlic and sauté, stirring, for 1 minute until fragrant. Add the turkey and steak seasoning. Cook, stirring frequently, until the turkey is browned on the edges (the turkey may not be completely cooked but will finish in the oven). Drain any accumulated juices.

4. Add the canned diced tomatoes, tomato paste, mustard, and relish, reduce the heat to medium, and stir until bubbling. Remove from the heat and stir in the drained pasta. Smooth the top. Cover the top of the casserole with the cheese slices, cutting as necessary to fit. Bake for 20 to 25 minutes until the cheese is melted and the mixture bubbles. Garnish with diced tomatoes, sprinkle with salt and pepper, and serve.

Unstuffed Cabbage Casserole

Yield: Serves 6 | Prep Time: 30 minutes | Cook Time: 55 minutes

Achieving the flavor profile of stuffed cabbage without the time spent carefully stuffing each leaf, this casserole is the best of both worlds. Cabbage is great for digestion, and with lean turkey protein you have a healthy casserole in the works. Bake and dig in, without stopping to worry about rolling things up or tying a bow on top.

INGREDIENTS

1 cup long-grain brown rice

2 tablespoons olive oil

1 cup chopped onion

2 garlic cloves, minced

1 (28-ounce) can diced tomatoes

½ cup tomato sauce

¼ cup chopped parsley

½ teaspoon salt

¼ teaspoon freshly ground black pepper

1 pound ground turkey

1 (2.5-pound) green cabbage

1 tablespoon light brown sugar

1 tablespoon red wine vinegar

½ teaspoon Worcestershire sauce

DIRECTIONS

1. Preheat the oven to 350°F and lightly coat a 9 × 13-inch baking dish with cooking spray.

2. Shred the cabbage, reserving 18 to 20 whole leaves for serving, if desired.

3. Cook the rice according to the package directions.

4. While the rice cooks, heat the olive oil in a large skillet over medium-high heat; add the onion and garlic and sauté for 2 minutes, until fragrant. Add the diced tomatoes, ½ of the tomato sauce, the parsley, salt, and pepper. Add the turkey and sauté for 5 minutes.

5. Add the shredded cabbage to the tomato sauce mixture and cook for 5 minutes to wilt the cabbage, stirring occasionally. Pour the mixture into the baking dish and bake for 45 minutes.

6. Meanwhile, add the brown sugar, vinegar, and Worcestershire sauce to the remaining tomato sauce in a small skillet and bring just to a simmer, stirring until well mixed. Pour the sauce over the baked casserole or serve on the side. Place 3 to 4 whole cabbage leaves in each individual bowl, top with casserole filling, and serve.

Chicken Breast–Salsa Verde Quesadilla Casserole

Yield: Serves 4 | Prep Time: 20 minutes | Cook Time: 35 minutes

Try this spicy dish for a Tex-Mex dinner that's a little lighter and brighter. Stringy cheese, salsa verde, and cilantro are packed between layers of tortillas and baked until just crisp enough to cut into. With whole-wheat tortillas, chicken breast meat, and reduced-fat cheese, it's a flavorful way to eat healthy.

INGREDIENTS

2 (7-ounce) cans salsa verde

1½ cups light sour cream

¼ cup chopped fresh cilantro, plus extra for serving

1 tablespoon finely chopped serrano chile

4 (6-inch) whole-wheat tortillas

4 cups shredded cooked chicken breast meat

3 scallions, thinly sliced

2 cups shredded reduced-fat white cheddar or Mexican-blend cheese, plus ¼ cup for serving

DIRECTIONS

1. Preheat the oven to 375°F and lightly coat a 9-inch cake pan or skillet with cooking spray.

2. In a medium bowl, mix the salsa verde with 1 cup of the sour cream, the cilantro, and chile until smooth.

3. Spoon one-quarter of the sauce into the pan. Place a tortilla on the sauce and add another quarter of the sauce. Add half of the chicken, half of the scallions, and half of the cheese. Repeat the layers: tortilla, sauce, chicken, scallions, and cheese. Add a third layer of tortillas and finish with the remaining sauce. Bake for 30 minutes. Top with remaining tortilla and ¼ cup of cheese. Return to the oven for 5 minutes. Serve with the remaining sour cream and fresh cilantro.

NOTES

To cook the chicken, place 4 boneless, skinless chicken breasts on a baking sheet and bake at 350°F for 30 minutes. Remove from the oven and shred.

Creamy Chicken and Kale Casserole

Yield: Serves 6 to 8 | Prep Time: 30 minutes | Cook Time: 45 minutes

A simple white sauce with whole-wheat penne and kale, this is one of my everyday favorites. The flavors are cheesy and adding a leafy green, like kale, is a fun way to incorporate healthy vegetables into your dinner routine. I love how it wilts slightly with the heat and surrounds the chicken for a creamy bite.

INGREDIENTS

1 (13.25-ounce) box whole-wheat penne

1 tablespoon unsalted butter

1 tablespoon olive oil

1 large onion, diced

1 garlic clove, minced

1½ pounds kale, stems removed, torn into bite-size pieces

32 ounces ricotta cheese

1 cup shredded mozzarella and provolone mixture or Italian cheese blend

¾ cup grated Pecorino Romano cheese

½ cup finely minced flat-leaf parsley

2 large eggs

1 tablespoon grated lemon zest

1 teaspoon kosher salt

½ teaspoon freshly ground black pepper

¼ teaspoon ground nutmeg

3 cups chopped or shredded cooked chicken breast meat

DIRECTIONS

1. Preheat the oven to 350°F and lightly coat a 9 × 13-inch baking dish with cooking spray.

2. Bring a large pot of water to a boil. Add the penne and cook until al dente, drain, and return to the pot.

3. Meanwhile, in a large skillet melt the butter and olive oil over medium heat. Add the onion and garlic and sauté for about 3 minutes, until soft. Add the kale, cover, and cook until the kale is slightly wilted, 5 to 7 minutes. Add the kale mixture to the pot with the pasta.

4. In a large bowl, mix the ricotta, other cheeses, parsley, eggs, lemon zest, salt, pepper, and nutmeg until well combined.

5. Add the chicken and the kale and pasta mixture and mix until well combined. Transfer to the baking dish and bake for 30 minutes until golden. Serve.

NOTES

To cook the chicken, place 3 boneless, skinless chicken breasts on a baking sheet and bake at 350°F for 30 minutes. Remove from the oven and shred or chop.

Yummy Pork Casserole

Yield: Serves 4 | Prep Time: 20 minutes | Cook Time: 1 hour 5 minutes

For a healthy and filling meal, this pork chop dish is wonderfully seasoned with herbs and spices. What I love about this dish is its simplicity, and the many sides that you can serve it with. Sometimes I plate this with broccoli, other times a salad, for a healthy and fast dinner. There is a time and place for unique flavors and bold cheeses, but sometimes you just want a simple dish, and this one is delightful.

INGREDIENTS

4 boneless pork chops, ½-inch thick

½ teaspoon salt

¼ teaspoon freshly ground black pepper

2 tablespoons vegetable oil

1 cup long-grain brown rice

2 (10-ounce) cans French onion soup

1 tablespoon minced fresh thyme, plus extra for serving

DIRECTIONS

1. Preheat the oven to 375°F and lightly coat an 8 × 8-inch or 11-inch round or square baking dish with cooking spray.

2. Season the pork chops with the salt and pepper. In a skillet large enough to hold all the chops, heat the oil over medium-high heat. Add the chops and sauté until brown on both sides, about 5 minutes total. (The chops do not need to be completely cooked—they will finish cooking in the oven later.)

3. Place the rice in the baking dish, add the soup, and stir to mix. Place the pork chops on top and sprinkle the thyme over the chops. Cover the baking dish tightly with foil or a lid and bake for 1 hour. Sprinkle with fresh thyme and serve.

Layered Smoked Sausage and Rice Casserole

Yield: Serves 6 to 8 | Prep Time: 30 minutes | Cook Time: 1 hour 10 minutes

Smoked sausage is one of my favorite sweet and spicy secret ingredients. Here it's folded into rice and baked with cabbage for a healthy but hearty dish. It's quite simple, and includes rice and tomatoes, cabbage and sausage—you get your grains, vegetables, and meat in one convenient casserole.

INGREDIENTS

1 tablespoon olive oil

1 onion, chopped

2 garlic cloves, minced

18 ounces smoked sausage, sliced ½-inch thick

1 (2.5-pound) head green cabbage, shredded (about 5 cups)

1 (15-ounce) can fire-roasted diced tomatoes

1 teaspoon dried thyme

½ teaspoon kosher salt

¼ teaspoon freshly ground black pepper

2 cups cooked long-grain brown rice

1 (15-ounce) can marinara sauce

1 cup shredded mozzarella

DIRECTIONS

1. Preheat the oven to 350°F and lightly coat a 9 × 13-inch baking dish with cooking spray.

2. In a large skillet, heat the olive oil over medium heat. Add the onion and garlic and sauté for 2 minutes. Add the sausage and cook, stirring, for 1 to 2 minutes. Add the shredded cabbage and cook for 5 minutes. Add the tomatoes, thyme, salt, and pepper and cook for 5 minutes. Add the cooked rice off the heat and stir to combine.

3. Pour the sausage mixture into the baking dish and pour the marinara sauce over the top. Cover with foil and bake for 40 to 45 minutes. Uncover, sprinkle with the cheese, and bake for an additional 10 minutes. Serve.

Spicy Shrimp and Rice Casserole

Yield: Serves 4 | Prep Time: 35 minutes | Cook Time: 35 minutes

Bell peppers and pepper Jack cheese help this shrimp dish pack a punch. Served with fiber-rich brown rice and infused with lemon juice, it is an easy meal for any day, low in calories, and high in good-for-you vegetables and protein.

INGREDIENTS

¼ cup olive oil

½ cup chopped red onion

½ cup chopped red bell pepper

½ cup chopped yellow bell pepper

½ cup scallions, sliced

4 garlic cloves, minced

1½ teaspoons kosher salt

½ teaspoon freshly ground black pepper

2 pounds large shrimp, peeled and deveined

3 cups cooked long-grain brown rice

½ cup dry white wine

1 tablespoon lemon juice

½ cup shredded pepper Jack cheese

¼ cup grated Parmesan cheese

DIRECTIONS

1. Preheat the oven to 350°F and lightly coat a 7 × 11-inch baking dish with cooking spray.

2. In a large skillet, heat the olive oil over medium heat. Add the onion and bell peppers and sauté for 6 to 8 minutes, until the vegetables start to soften. Add the scallions and garlic and sauté for 1 to 2 minutes, then stir in the salt and pepper. Add the shrimp and cook until the shrimp turn pink and are cooked. Add the rice, wine, and lemon juice and stir to combine.

3. Pour into the baking dish and sprinkle the pepper Jack and Parmesan over the top. Bake for 20 minutes, or until the cheeses are melted and the top is bubbling. Serve.

Sweet Potato and Sausage Casserole

Yield: Serves 6 to 8 | Prep Time: 30 minutes | Cook Time: 55 minutes

A sweet twist on meat and potatoes, this sweet potato sausage casserole is a nice change from routine dinners. It's a healthier option thanks to the nutrient-packed sweet potato, making it another good choice to add to your recipe box.

INGREDIENTS

6 sweet potatoes, unpeeled

4 tablespoons olive oil

2 teaspoons salt

2 teaspoons freshly ground black pepper

1 onion, diced

6 garlic cloves, minced

1 pound hot Italian sausage, casings removed

1 cup grated Parmesan cheese

1 teaspoon crushed red pepper flakes (optional)

DIRECTIONS

1. Preheat the oven to 400°F and lightly coat a 9 × 13-inch baking dish with cooking spray.

2. Cut the sweet potatoes into large cubes and toss with 2 tablespoons of the olive oil, the salt, and the pepper. Transfer to the baking dish and roast for 30 minutes.

3. Meanwhile, in a large skillet, heat the remaining oil over medium heat. Add the onion and garlic and sauté for 5 minutes. Add the sausage and break apart with a wooden spoon until cooked.

4. Add the sausage to the sweet potatoes and top with the Parmesan and pepper flakes, if using. Bake for another 15 minutes. Serve.

30-Minute Shrimp Bake

Yield: Serves 6 | Prep Time: 15 minutes | Cook Time: 15 minutes

If you're in the mood for seafood, this shrimp bake is easy to execute and sure to hit the spot. Sautéed shrimp with a rich tomato sauce served over rice is a nice way to mix things up during the week. Most of shrimp's calories come from protein, and they contain plenty of omega-3 fatty acids to make for a healthier weeknight dinner.

INGREDIENTS

1 lemon

1 bay leaf

6 black peppercorns

2 teaspoons salt

1 pound medium shrimp, shelled and deveined

4 cups cooked long-grain brown rice

1 (10.75-ounce) can cream of mushroom soup

1 (10.75-ounce) can cheddar cheese soup

1 cup shredded low-fat pepper Jack or Monterey Jack cheese

2 teaspoons lemon pepper seasoning

DIRECTIONS

1. Preheat the oven to 350°F and lightly coat a 9 × 13-inch baking dish with cooking spray.

2. Grate 1 teaspoon zest from the lemon and set aside, then cut the lemon into 8 wedges.

3. In a large pot, bring 5 cups water to a boil with the bay leaf, peppercorns, and 1 teaspoon of the salt. Drop 2 of the lemon wedges into the water, add the shrimp, and boil for 2 to 3 minutes, until the shrimp begin to turn pink. Drain the shrimp and discard the lemon and peppercorns. Reserve the bay leaf for garnish, if desired.

4. In a large bowl, combine the cooked rice and shrimp and stir in the soups, half of the cheese, the lemon pepper seasoning, lemon zest, and remaining 1 teaspoon salt. Spoon into the baking dish and sprinkle with the remaining cheese. Cover with foil and bake for 15 minutes, until the cheese is melted and the mixture is heated through. Serve with the remaining lemon wedges.

Creamy Tuna Shell Casserole

Yield: Serves 6 to 8 | Prep Time: 30 minutes | Cook Time: 30 minutes

When I pair seafood with pasta, I always use shells. Can you guess why? You're right, the ocean. I know, slightly cheesy, no (second) pun intended there, but why not? Not only am I a sucker for an edible pun, but I love when the shells envelop the tuna filling, delivering each bite straight to your mouth!

INGREDIENTS

6 ounces jumbo pasta shells

¼ cup olive oil

1 red bell pepper, sliced

3 (6-ounce) cans tuna, drained

5 ounces baby spinach

1 teaspoon crushed red pepper flakes

1 (28-ounce) jar Alfredo sauce

1 cup dried bread crumbs

¼ cup chopped scallions

DIRECTIONS

1. Preheat the oven to 375°F. Lightly coat a 9 × 13-inch baking dish with cooking spray.

2. Bring a large pot of water to a boil, add the pasta shells, and cook until al dente. Drain and reserve.

3. While the pasta cooks, in a large saucepan, heat 3 tablespoons of the olive oil over medium heat, add the bell pepper and sauté until soft.

4. Add the tuna, spinach, and pepper flakes and cook, stirring, for 2 minutes.

5. Add the cooked pasta and Alfredo sauce and stir. Pour the mixture into the baking dish. Top with the bread crumbs, drizzle with the remaining 1 tablespoon olive oil, and bake for 20 minutes. Top with scallions and serve.

Pork Chop Ranch Casserole

Yield: Serves 6 to 8 | Prep Time: 20 minutes | Cook Time: 1 hour 15 minutes

These thin roasted red potatoes almost taste like potato chips, with perfectly seared pork tucked in and baked with zesty ranch flavor. Pork chops haven't always been my go-to protein, but this dish has earned its spot in my dinner rotation.

INGREDIENTS

1 cup panko bread crumbs

¾ cup bottled ranch dressing

¼ cup all-purpose flour

6 boneless pork chops, ¾ inch thick

1 tablespoon vegetable oil

2 cups half-and-half

1 teaspoon salt

½ teaspoon freshly ground black pepper

2½ pounds small red potatoes, unpeeled, very thinly sliced

3 garlic cloves, thinly sliced

2 tablespoons chopped fresh chives

DIRECTIONS

1. Preheat the oven to 350°F and lightly coat a 9 × 13-inch baking dish with cooking spray.

2. Place the panko, dressing, and flour in separate shallow dishes or pie plates.

3. Dredge the pork chops in the flour, shaking off the excess, then dip into the dressing to coat; finally, dredge in the panko. In a large skillet, heat the oil over medium-high heat, add the pork chops, and cook for 3 to 4 minutes per side until golden brown on both sides. (The chops do not need to be fully cooked; they will finish in the oven.)

4. Place the chops in a medium saucepan with the half-and-half, salt, and pepper and bring to a boil. Reduce the heat but allow the mixture to bubble constantly for 5 minutes, stirring frequently so it does not stick to the bottom.

5. Pour the potatoes into the baking dish and tuck the pork chops into the potatoes with the garlic. Cover with foil and bake for 1 hour. Remove the foil and check that the potatoes are tender; if not, return to the oven for another 5 to 10 minutes. Serve, topped with fresh chives.

7

Internationally Inspired

I love to travel, and have been fortunate to do so. Whether from

the local Spanish market or all the way from Italy, flavors inspired

by different regions and countries always excite me in the

kitchen. I've adapted and experimented with some of my favorite

recipes to bring my vacation memories to life in a meal.

Layered Enchilada Casserole

Yield: Serves 4 | Prep Time: 20 minutes | Cook Time: 20 minutes

Bold flavors and culinary style make Mexican cuisine a favorite in my house. Not only do my husband and I enjoy fiestas for two on plenty of date nights, but it's safe to say we eat Mexican-inspired food at least twice a week. There are so many fresh ingredients to include, enhanced by vibrant spices.

INGREDIENTS

1 pound lean ground beef

1 packet taco seasoning

1 (15-ounce) can black beans, rinsed and drained

1 (10-ounce) can red enchilada sauce

½ cup sour cream

4 (6-inch) corn tortillas

1 cup shredded Mexican cheese blend

Fresh cilantro, for garnish

DIRECTIONS

1. Preheat the oven to 375°F and lightly coat an 8 × 8-inch baking dish with cooking spray.

2. In a large skillet, cook the ground beef with the taco seasoning over medium heat, stirring to break up the meat, until no longer pink.

3. Add the beans and half of the enchilada sauce and stir to combine.

4. Spread the sour cream over the 4 tortillas, then top all 4 with the beef and bean mixture and ½ cup cheese. Roll up each tortilla and place them side by side in the baking dish. Top with the remaining enchilada sauce and remaining cheese. Bake for 20 minutes. Serve, garnished with fresh cilantro.

Individual Tamale Pies

Yield: Serves 6 to 8 | Prep Time: 40 minutes | Cook Time: 25 minutes

I love serving food to a crowd of friends watching a game or awards show on television. These pies are a fun twist on traditional appetizers and are supereasy to make. Assembled in mini ramekins and put out for people to grab, the pies' cornmeal crust bottoms are slightly salty and soak up the tomatoes and beef, which are perfectly paired with corn and peppers and topped with spicy jalapeños and cheese. It's a complete meal in a compact form.

INGREDIENTS

1 (15.25-ounce) can whole kernel corn, drained

1 cup cornmeal

4 tablespoons unsalted butter, melted

¼ cup olive oil

2 pounds ground beef

1 onion, diced

2 jalapeño peppers, seeds removed and sliced

1 teaspoon salt

1 teaspoon freshly ground black pepper

1 (28-ounce) can diced tomatoes

1 cup shredded cheddar cheese

Fresh cilantro, for garnish

DIRECTIONS

1. Preheat the oven to 375°F and lightly coat six 8- to 12-ounce ramekins with cooking spray.

2. Combine the corn, cornmeal, and melted butter in a bowl. Press the mixture into the bottoms of the ramekins and place on a baking sheet.

3. In a large skillet, heat the olive oil over medium heat. Add the ground beef, onion, jalapeños, salt, and pepper and cook, stirring to break up the meat, until the meat is no longer pink. Add the tomatoes and cheese and stir to combine.

4. Divide the beef mixture among the ramekins and bake for 20 minutes, until warmed through. Serve, garnished with fresh cilantro.

Fried Rice Teriyaki Casserole

Yield: Serves 6 to 8 | Prep Time: 20 minutes | Cook Time: 50 minutes

Teriyaki is actually the name of a cooking technique originating in Japan in which foods are broiled or grilled with a sweet and salty soy sauce–based glaze. This casserole combines all the flavors of ginger, soy, and sesame oil in one big rice bowl, served piping hot with peas, chicken, and broccoli. The sesame seeds that coat the sweet glaze add crunch from the first bite.

INGREDIENTS

Teriyaki Sauce and Chicken

¾ cup low-sodium soy sauce

½ cup plus 2 tablespoons cold water

⅓ cup light brown sugar

1 tablespoon honey

1 teaspoon sesame oil

1 garlic clove, minced

½ teaspoon grated fresh ginger

2 tablespoons cornstarch

4 boneless, skinless chicken breasts

Fried Rice

2 tablespoons sesame oil

1 tablespoon unsalted butter

3 large eggs

3 cups cooked long-grain white rice

1 (10-ounce) package frozen stir-fry vegetables (broccoli, carrots, snow peas, water chestnuts)

3 scallions, chopped

½ teaspoon sesame seeds, toasted

DIRECTIONS

1. Preheat the oven to 350°F. Lightly coat a 9 × 13-inch baking dish with cooking spray.

2. For the teriyaki sauce and chicken: In a large saucepan, combine the soy sauce, ½ cup of the water, the sugar, honey, sesame oil, garlic, and ginger and bring to a boil. Cook for 2 minutes, stirring occasionally.

3. In a small bowl, combine the cornstarch and remaining 2 tablespoons water to create a slurry. Add 1 teaspoon of the hot soy mixture to the slurry. Pour the slurry into the remaining soy mixture. Whisk until thickened and remove from the heat.

4. Place the chicken in the prepared baking dish and pour 1 cup of the teriyaki sauce over the chicken. Set the remaining sauce aside. Bake for 30 minutes, or until the chicken is fully cooked.

5. For the fried rice: While the chicken cooks, heat the oil and butter in a large skillet over medium heat. Drop the eggs into the skillet and cook, stirring with a spatula, until the eggs are scrambled. Add the cooked rice and cook for 2 to 3 minutes. Set aside.

6. Remove the chicken from the oven, place on a baking sheet, and shred with a fork and knife.

7. Mix together the vegetables, rice, and chicken and add them to an 8 × 8-inch baking dish. Add 3 tablespoons of the reserved teriyaki sauce and stir to combine. Bake for 15 minutes. Drizzle with additional sauce and sprinkle with scallions and sesame seeds. Serve.

Beef and Broccoli Take-Out Fake-Out

Yield: Serves 6 to 8 | Prep Time: 30 minutes | Cook Time: 45 minutes

Love carry-out Chinese beef and broccoli, but hoping to make it at home? Here is an easy way to make and serve this restaurant favorite that avoids all of the last-minute flurry and frying of most DIY versions. Do all of the prep, measuring, and frying up to 12 hours ahead of time and then just pop the casserole in the oven to heat it up before serving. Even faster than waiting for delivery!

INGREDIENTS

2 cups long-grain white rice

4 cups water

1¼ teaspoons sesame oil

2 tablespoons soy sauce

2 tablespoons rice wine

2 tablespoons cornstarch

½ teaspoon crushed red pepper flakes

2 pounds round steak

1 cup beef or chicken broth

2 teaspoons rice wine vinegar

2 tablespoons peanut oil

2 large garlic cloves, minced

1 teaspoon grated fresh ginger

4 scallions, sliced

4 cups broccoli florets, cooked

1 (8-ounce) can water chestnuts, drained well

Fried chow mein noodles

Toasted sesame seeds

DIRECTIONS

1. Preheat the oven to 350°F and lightly coat a 9 × 13-inch baking dish with cooking spray.

2. Combine the rice, water, and ¼ teaspoon of the sesame oil in a small saucepan, bring to a boil, cover, and simmer until the water has evaporated and the rice is cooked, about 20 minutes. Fluff with a fork and set aside.

3. Combine 1 tablespoon of the soy sauce, 1 tablespoon of the rice wine, 1 tablespoon of the cornstarch, and the pepper flakes in a medium bowl, mixing well.

4. Slice the steak into 1-inch strips. Add it to the soy sauce mixture and stir to coat well. Let stand for 10 minutes.

5. Meanwhile, in a second bowl, combine the broth, rice wine vinegar, the remaining soy sauce and sesame oil, rice wine, and cornstarch. Set aside.

6. In a large, deep skillet or wok heat the peanut oil over high heat; add the garlic and ginger and cook, stirring, until fragrant, about 1 minute. Add the steak and scallions and cook, tossing constantly, until the steak is browned on the edges. Add the broth mixture and cook, stirring, until the sauce is thickened. Stir in the broccoli and water chestnuts.

7. Pour the steak mixture into the baking dish. Top with the rice in an even layer, cover very tightly with foil, and bake for 20 to 25 minutes just to warm through. Sprinkle the chow mein noodles and sesame seeds over the top and serve.

Italian Layer Bake

Yield: Serves 4 | Prep Time: 15 minutes | Cook Time: 40 minutes

My husband and I went to Italy a few years ago and spent much of our time seeking out the perfect panini. We became a bit spoiled from finding hot, fresh sandwiches on every street corner, and upon returning home we did our best to replicate them. They vary in ingredients, but one thing's for sure: regular cold cut sandwiches seem boring compared to these hot, melted delights. In this casserole version, roasted red peppers peek out of the multiple layers of ham, turkey, and Swiss cheese. Crescent rolls act as the bread, holding it all together until you dive in with a fork and watch as the egg and Dijon mustard seep through, adding extra flavor to every crevice.

INGREDIENTS

2 (8-ounce) tubes refrigerated original-style crescent rolls

2 tablespoons Dijon mustard

8 ounces sliced turkey

8 ounces sliced honey ham

8 ounces sliced salami

1 pound Swiss cheese, sliced

1 (12-ounce) jar roasted red peppers

4 large eggs, lightly beaten

DIRECTIONS

1. Preheat the oven to 350°F and lightly coat an 8 × 8-inch baking dish with cooking spray.

2. Unroll 1 tube of crescent rolls and place in the baking dish in 1 piece. Use your fingers to press together all the seams and make an even layer of dough in the bottom and partially up the sides of the dish. Dollop with 1 tablespoon of the mustard and spread across the dough (this will be messy).

3. Top with half of the turkey, ham, salami, cheese, and roasted peppers. Pour half of the beaten eggs on top.

4. Add the remaining turkey, ham, salami, cheese, and roasted peppers in the same order and top with the remaining crescent dough. Brush with the remaining beaten eggs, cover with foil, and bake for 20 minutes. Remove the foil and bake for an additional 20 minutes, until golden. Serve.

Cheesy Chicken Alfredo Casserole

Yield: Serves 6 to 8 | Prep Time: 20 minutes, plus 30 minutes to 8 hours to marinate | Cook Time: 50 minutes

Traditionally in Italy, Alfredo is a pasta dish made with fettuccine. Melted Parmesan cheese and butter emulsify with cream to form a smooth coating. With some extra Italian seasoning and cubed chicken, this baked dish is as comforting as it is tasty.

INGREDIENTS

2 pounds boneless, skinless chicken breasts, cut into bite-size pieces

½ cup Italian salad dressing

1 teaspoon Italian seasoning

1 pound fettuccine

2 tablespoons olive oil

1 tablespoon finely minced garlic

8 tablespoons unsalted butter

3 tablespoons all-purpose flour

3 cups half-and-half

2 ounces cream cheese, room temperature

2 cups shredded Italian cheese blend

1 cup grated Parmesan cheese

Salt and freshly ground black pepper

DIRECTIONS

1. Toss the chicken, salad dressing, and Italian seasoning together and allow to stand for at least 30 minutes or up to 8 hours refrigerated.

2. Preheat the oven to 350°F and lightly coat a 9 × 13-inch baking dish with cooking spray.

3. Bring a large pot of salted water to a boil, add the fettuccine, and cook until al dente. Drain and return it to the pot.

4. In a large skillet, heat the olive oil over medium-high heat. Add the chicken and garlic and sauté, stirring often, until the chicken is lightly cooked, about 5 minutes. Using a slotted spoon, transfer to the pot with the cooked pasta and toss to combine.

5. In the empty skillet, melt the butter over medium heat and whisk in the flour, cooking and whisking constantly for 1 minute until the mixture is foamy and light-colored. Stir in the half-and-half and cream cheese and whisk until the sauce is thickened, about 4 minutes. Toss with the pasta and chicken, adding 1 cup of the Italian cheese blend and ½ cup of the Parmesan. Add salt and pepper to taste.

6. Pour into the baking dish and top with the remaining cheese blend and finally the remaining Parmesan. Bake for 30 minutes, until bubbling and the top is golden brown. Serve.

Beef Stroganoff Casserole

Yield: Serves 6 to 8 | Prep Time: 20 minutes | Cook Time: 1 hour

This traditional Russian dish, which originated in the nineteenth century, has changed a bit over the years, but not much. My twist on the classic is the noodle combination. I love egg noodles paired with fusilli, as the dual textures make for a more interesting mouthfeel and a festive presentation.

INGREDIENTS

8 ounces medium egg noodles

8 ounces fusilli

1 pound lean ground beef

12 ounces white button mushrooms, sliced

4 garlic cloves, minced

2½ cups water

1 cup sour cream

2 (1-ounce) packets beef gravy mix

1 teaspoon freshly ground black pepper

½ teaspoon ground nutmeg

DIRECTIONS

1. Preheat the oven to 375°F and lightly coat a 9 × 13-inch casserole dish with cooking spray.

2. Bring a large pot of water to a boil, add the egg noodles, and cook until al dente. Using a skimmer, transfer the noodles to a colander to drain. Return the water to a boil, add the fusilli, and cook until al dente. Drain and reserve.

3. In a large skillet, sauté the beef, mushrooms, and garlic, stirring to break up the meat, until the meat is no longer pink. Add the water, sour cream, gravy mix, pepper, and nutmeg and stir to combine.

4. Stir in the noodles and fusilli and pour into the baking dish. Bake for 40 minutes. Serve.

Hearty Burrito Casserole

Yield: Serves 6 to 8 | Prep Time: 25 minutes | Cook Time: 35 minutes

My husband is a big fan of the bowl or burrito from his favorite fast-casual Mexican food place. On days when I don't feel like eating out, this is my go-to alternative to satisfy that craving without leaving the house. If you love the elements that make a big burrito, this one's for you: it's cheesy, packed with beans and beef, and topped with crispy tortillas.

INGREDIENTS

1 tablespoon vegetable oil

1 cup chopped onion

1½ pounds lean ground beef

½ cup chopped fresh cilantro

1 (1-ounce) packet taco seasoning

1 (10.75-ounce) can cheddar cheese soup

½ cup salsa

¼ cup sour cream

8 (8-inch) flour tortillas, cut into strips

1 (16-ounce) can refried beans

2 cups shredded Mexican cheese blend

DIRECTIONS

1. Preheat the oven to 350°F and lightly coat a 9 × 13-inch baking dish with cooking spray.

2. In a large skillet, heat the oil over medium-high heat; add the onion and sauté for 2 minutes, until translucent. Add the ground beef and cook, stirring to break up the meat, for 4 to 5 minutes until the meat is no longer pink. Stir in the cilantro and taco seasoning and cook for 2 minutes.

3. In a small bowl, combine the soup, salsa, and sour cream. Spread 1 cup of the mixture into the bottom of the baking dish. Top with half of the tortilla strips in a flat layer. Spread the refried beans over the tortillas in a smooth layer. Add half of the meat mixture, topped with half of the cheese. Spread the remaining soup mixture on top of the cheese and top with the remaining meat mixture and the remaining tortilla strips. Sprinkle the remaining cheese over the top.

4. Bake for 25 minutes, until the mixture is bubbling and the cheese is melted. Serve.

Pierogi Casserole

Yield: Serves 6 to 8 | Prep Time: 1 hour | Cook Time: 1 hour 15 minutes

Of all the Polish foods that Martha Stewart loves, pierogi are her favorite. I spent a few years working for her, and I remember when they were made for a holiday party. As she has always been a role model to me, I think of Martha when I make them, too. My take is a bit different: layered like a lasagna and topped with bacon, the flavors and textures will remind you of traditional pierogi, but put together in the most convenient way!

INGREDIENTS

10 lasagna noodles, regular or no-boil

3½ pounds Yukon Gold potatoes, peeled and cut into chunks

5 tablespoons unsalted butter

1 tablespoon olive oil

2 onions, sliced

Pinch sugar

½ cup whole milk

½ cup half-and-half

½ cup sour cream

1 teaspoon kosher salt

½ teaspoon freshly ground black pepper

4 cups shredded sharp cheddar cheese

2 cups ricotta cheese, drained

8 ounces bacon, cooked and crumbled

DIRECTIONS

1. Preheat the oven to 375°F.

2. If using regular lasagna noodles, bring a large pot of water to a boil, add the noodles, and cook until al dente. (If using no-boil noodles, skip this step.) Drain and rinse, place on a lightly greased baking sheet, and cover until ready to use.

3. Bring a large pot of salted water to a boil, add the potatoes, and cook until tender, about 30 minutes.

4. While the potatoes are cooking, heat 1 tablespoon of the butter and the olive oil in a large skillet, add the onions and sugar, and sauté until the onions are golden and caramelized.

5. Drain the potatoes. Mash with remaining 4 tablespoons butter, the milk, half-and-half, sour cream, salt, and pepper until smooth. Mix in 3 cups of the cheddar.

6. Place 4 lasagna noodles on the bottom of the baking dish. Top with 1 cup of the ricotta. Spread one-third of the potato mixture on top of the ricotta. Spread one-third of the onions and one-third of the bacon over the potato mixture. Set 3 noodles on the bacon and top with the remaining ricotta, then layer with another third of the potato mixture, onions, and bacon. Place the last 3 noodles on top, then the remaining potato mixture, onions, and bacon.

7. Top with the remaining cheddar and bake for 30 minutes, or until golden. Serve.

Layered Chicken Spaghetti Italian Casserole

Yield: Serves 6 | Prep Time: 30 minutes | Cook Time: 40 minutes

My Sunday supper favorite, this spaghetti casserole is easy to make and enjoy with a warm baguette, a green salad with a light vinaigrette, and a glass of red wine. This will make any date night at home feel like dinner at a four-star restaurant and bring your weekend to a cozy close.

INGREDIENTS

8 ounces thin spaghetti

2 cups chopped cooked chicken

2 (10.75-ounce) cans cream of mushroom soup

1 (10-ounce) can diced tomatoes

1 cup sour cream

¼ teaspoon freshly ground black pepper

1 cup shredded Italian cheese blend

2 tablespoons grated Parmesan cheese

1 cup Italian-style bread crumbs

2 tablespoons unsalted butter, melted

DIRECTIONS

1. Preheat the oven to 350°F and lightly coat a 9 × 13-inch baking dish with cooking spray.

2. Bring a large pot of water to a boil, add the spaghetti, and cook until al dente. Drain and return to the pot. Add the chicken, soup, tomatoes, sour cream, and pepper, and stir to combine. Transfer to the baking dish, cover with foil, and bake for 30 minutes. Remove the foil, and sprinkle both cheeses over the top, then sprinkle the bread crumbs over the cheese.

3. Drizzle the melted butter over the bread crumbs, return to the oven, and bake until the cheeses have melted and the bread crumb topping is golden brown. Serve.

NOTES

To cook the chicken: place 2 medium boneless, skinless chicken breasts on a baking sheet and bake at 350°F for 30 minutes. Remove from the oven and shred.

Ground Beef Pastitsio

Yield: Serves 6 to 8 | Prep Time: 15 minutes | Cook Time: 1 hour

When my husband and I first started dating, he didn't like onions or garlic. As I began my mission to convince him of the deliciousness he was missing out on, I found a recipe for pastitsio for two. I used ground lamb, as in the classic Greek recipe, and over the years this recipe has evolved and become a staple in our home, usually with beef replacing the lamb.

INGREDIENTS

Pastitsio

1 pound elbow macaroni or cavatappi

4 tablespoons unsalted butter

1 onion, diced

4 garlic cloves, minced

1 pound lean ground beef

Salt and freshly ground black pepper

1 teaspoon dried oregano

2 cups tomato sauce

1 cup shredded provolone cheese

Béchamel Sauce

2 tablespoons unsalted butter

2 tablespoons all-purpose flour

1¼ cups whole milk, warm

Salt and freshly ground black pepper

¼ teaspoon crushed red pepper

1 tablespoon chopped fresh parsley

DIRECTIONS

1. Preheat the oven to 350°F. Lightly coat a 9 × 13-inch baking dish with cooking spray.

2. Bring a large pot of salted water to a boil and cook the pasta until al dente. Drain and reserve.

3. In a large skillet, melt the butter over medium heat. Add the onions and garlic and sauté until tender. Add the ground beef and cook, stirring to break up the meat, until no longer pink. Add the salt, pepper, and oregano and remove from the heat.

4. Spread ¼ cup of the tomato sauce in the baking dish and top with half of the cooked pasta.

5. Top with the meat and the remaining sauce. Cover with the provolone and the remaining pasta.

6. For the béchamel: Melt the butter in a small saucepan over medium heat. Stir in the flour and cook, stirring, to form a paste. Add the milk and continue to stir as the sauce thickens, 2 to 3 minutes. Season with salt and pepper to taste.

7. Cover the casserole with the béchamel sauce and bake for 40 minutes. Serve, topped with crushed red pepper and chopped parsley.

Easy Baked Goulash

Yield: Serves 4 | Prep Time: 20 minutes | Cook Time: 50 minutes

This dish is one of my favorites. Not because it is super simple, but because a little while back I competed on a television show called *Cutthroat Kitchen*. This show, on the Food Network, is a wacky one. There are obstacles and time restraints, themes and sabotages, and you still need to cook delicious food. I was challenged to make traditional Hungarian goulash, and this recipe is quite close to the one that I made on TV, a dish that led me to a final round, which I ended up winning! It's a one-pot wonder that has enough Hungarian paprika to pack a punch and plenty of mushrooms and crazy corkscrew noodles.

INGREDIENTS

2 tablespoons olive oil

8 ounces white button mushrooms, sliced

1 onion, diced

6 garlic cloves, minced

2 pounds lean ground beef

1 (28-ounce) jar marinara sauce

8 ounces elbow macaroni or cavatappi

½ cup water

1 tablespoon paprika

1 teaspoon salt

1 teaspoon freshly ground black pepper

DIRECTIONS

1. Preheat the oven to 350°F and lightly coat a 9 × 13-inch baking dish with cooking spray.

2. In a large skillet, add 2 tablespoons of olive oil. Sauté the mushrooms, onion, and garlic over medium heat. Add the ground beef and cook, stirring to break up the meat, until no longer pink. Add the marinara, pasta, water, paprika, salt, and pepper.

3. Pour into the baking dish.

4. Bake for 45 minutes. Serve.

8

Dessert

People often ask whether I love cooking or baking more. My answer varies from day to day, depending on my mood, but after making the recipes in this chapter, I may favor baking! From frozen desserts to warm and gooey cakes, these are dessert casseroles you just have to try. They are easy, elegant, and perfect for kids, adults, parties, or just for you.

Whipped Cookie Delight

Yield: Serves 10 to 12 | Prep Time: 20 minutes | Cook Time: 15 minutes, refrigerate 30 minutes

This recipe is like a magic trick. How can three layers with very few ingredients turn into something so divine? I would argue it's the multitextural component: a cookie bottom topped with light fluffy cream, followed by a denser pudding and topped with crunchy chips. It is elegant and delicious, but beyond easy!

INGREDIENTS

1 (16-ounce) package refrigerated chocolate chip cookie dough, room temperature

8 ounces cream cheese, room temperature

1 cup powdered sugar

1 (8-ounce) container whipped topping

1 (3.4-ounce) box instant chocolate pudding mix

1 (3.4-ounce) box instant vanilla pudding mix

3 cups whole milk, cold

Mini chocolate chips, for topping

DIRECTIONS

1. Preheat the oven to 350°F. Lightly coat a 9 × 13-inch baking dish with cooking spray and line it with parchment paper.

2. Spread the cookie dough evenly over the bottom of the baking dish and bake for 15 minutes, until golden brown. Let cool completely.

3. In a medium bowl, mix together the cream cheese and powdered sugar. Fold in the whipped topping. Spread the cream cheese mixture over the cooled cookie base.

4. Combine the chocolate and vanilla puddings with the milk in a large bowl and whisk until smooth. Let stand for 2 minutes, then spread on top of the cream cheese layer. Top with mini chocolate chips and refrigerate for at least 30 minutes before serving.

NOTES

Experiment with pudding flavors! Instead of vanilla, try white chocolate or banana.

Ice Cream Sandwich Casserole

Yield: Serves 6 to 8 | Prep Time: 10 minutes | Refrigerate: 1 hour

My husband joked that my casserole enthusiasm was slightly out of hand when I made a casserole out of ice cream sandwiches. He thought it was funny and indulgent, but then he tried it. Stacked together with layers of hot fudge and caramel, sliced into a perfect cake piece, and topped with whipped topping—this is how you eat an ice cream sandwich! Everyone's favorite summer poolside treat is now a decadent casserole for any occasion.

INGREDIENTS

24 ice cream sandwiches

1 (12-ounce) jar hot fudge topping

1 (12-ounce) jar caramel topping

1 (8-ounce) container whipped topping

1 (8-ounce) bag toffee chips

DIRECTIONS

1. Arrange 1 layer of ice cream sandwiches in the bottom of a 9 × 13-inch baking dish, cutting the sandwiches to fit if needed.

2. Melt the hot fudge and spread a layer on top of the sandwiches, using half of the fudge in the jar. Repeat with half of the caramel.

3. Top with half of the whipped topping and sprinkle half of the toffee chips on top.

4. Repeat with the remaining sandwiches, remaining sauces, toffee chips, and whipped topping.

5. Cover and place in the freezer for an hour, until solid. Serve.

Crushed Pineapple Cake Casserole

Yield: Serves 6 | Prep Time: 5 minutes | Cook Time: 30 minutes

I absolutely love the colors of this crushed pineapple casserole. Sweet tangy pineapple looks as bright as the sun and is the fastest way to make a unique yellow cake. It's like a pineapple upside-down cake, but in casserole form!

INGREDIENTS

1 (15.25-ounce) box yellow cake mix

3 (20-ounce) cans crushed pineapple, drained

2 bananas, sliced

½ cup sugar

DIRECTIONS

1. Preheat the oven to 375°F and lightly coat an 8-inch skillet or cake pan with cooking spray.

2. Combine the cake mix with 2 cans of the pineapple and pour into the skillet. Pour the remaining can over the top.

3. Add the sliced bananas, sprinkle the sugar evenly over the bananas, and bake for 30 minutes. Serve.

Deep-Dish Chocolate Chip Pie

Yield: Serves 8 | Prep Time: 15 minutes | Cook Time: 1 hour

I was caught red-handed eating this for breakfast the other day. You may find yourself doing the same! The deep-dish chocolate cookie deliciousness paired with vanilla bean ice cream and topped with walnuts and chocolate chips will stare you in the eye until the last crumb has been consumed, no matter the time of day.

INGREDIENTS

2 large eggs

½ cup all-purpose flour

½ cup granulated sugar

½ cup packed light brown sugar

12 tablespoons unsalted butter, room temperature

1½ cups semisweet chocolate chips, plus extra for serving

1 unbaked 9-inch deep-dish pie shell

1 cup walnuts, plus extra for serving, chopped

Vanilla bean ice cream

DIRECTIONS

1. Preheat the oven to 350°F.

2. In the bowl of a stand mixer, beat the eggs on high speed until light and foamy. Add the flour and both sugars and beat until combined. Add the butter and beat until completely mixed. Mix in the chocolate chips. Pour the batter into the pie crust and top with the walnuts.

3. Bake for 1 hour. Let cool slightly.

4. Serve warm with vanilla bean ice cream, chocolate chips, and walnuts.

NOTES

If you're allergic to nuts, omit them; it will taste just as delicious!

Delightful Donut Casserole

Yield: Serves 8 | Prep Time: 10 minutes | Cook Time: 20 to 30 minutes

I absolutely love donuts. I am famous for my pumpkin donut recipe, I own a pair of pants with donuts on them, and instead of a wedding cake, my husband and I served up hot, fresh assorted fried donuts! So when there is a way to combine them with more cinnamon and butter, sign me up!

INGREDIENTS

Casserole

1 (15-ounce) box donut holes

6 tablespoons unsalted butter, melted

¼ cup light brown sugar

1 large egg

½ teaspoon ground cinnamon

½ teaspoon vanilla extract

Topping

½ cup all-purpose flour

½ cup light brown sugar

¼ cup granulated sugar

4 tablespoons unsalted butter, melted

1 teaspoon ground cinnamon

DIRECTIONS

1. Preheat the oven to 350°F and lightly coat an 8 × 8-inch baking dish with cooking spray.

2. For the casserole: Place the donut holes in the baking dish. Combine the butter, sugar, egg, cinnamon, and vanilla in a small bowl and sprinkle over the donut holes.

3. Bake for 20 minutes.

4. For the topping: While the casserole bakes, combine all the ingredients in a small bowl.

5. Remove the casserole from the oven and top with the sugar mixture. Bake for another 10 minutes until golden. Let cool slightly before serving.

NOTES

Mix it up with different donut flavors, like chocolate or pumpkin.

Make-Ahead Nutty Cookie Lasagna

Yield: Serves 6 | Prep Time: 10 minutes | Refrigerate overnight

This looks and tastes like a cloud—a peanut butter cookie cloud, that is! Once assembled and left to chill overnight, the cookies absorb some of the whipped topping and your fork will cruise right through the cloud of fluff. It will take you 10 minutes to make, and the same amount of time for everyone to devour it.

INGREDIENTS

1 (16-ounce) box peanut butter sandwich cookies

1 cup creamy peanut butter, melted

1 (3.4-ounce) box instant vanilla pudding mix

1 (8-ounce) container whipped topping

DIRECTIONS

1. Line the bottom of an 8 × 8-inch baking dish with cookies.

2. Top with half of the melted peanut butter and sprinkle half of the pudding powder over the peanut butter.

3. Add half of the whipped topping.

4. Repeat with another layer of cookies and the remaining peanut butter, pudding powder, and whipped topping. Crush the remaining peanut butter cookies and sprinkle over the top.

5. Cover and refrigerate overnight. Serve.

20-Minute Chocolate Candy Cookie Casserole

Yield: Serves 6 | Prep Time: 10 minutes | Freeze for 10 minutes

Until I discovered this recipe, I hadn't had a chocolate candy cookie sandwich in a very long time. Now, I can't seem to stop making this casserole! As the ice cream melts, it soaks through the soft cookies, making them even chewier. Topped with more chocolate candies for a crunch, it is the brightest-colored candy dessert I have seen.

INGREDIENTS

1 (8-ounce) container whipped topping

2 (24-ounce) boxes chocolate candy cookie ice cream sandwiches

1 cup hot fudge topping

Candy-coated chocolate candies, like M&M's

DIRECTIONS

1. Spread the whipped topping on the bottom of an 8 × 8-inch baking dish.

2. Cut the ice cream sandwiches in half and place them round-side down on the whipped topping.

3. In the microwave, heat the hot fudge topping for 30 seconds to warm. Drizzle the fudge topping over the sandwiches and top with the chocolate candies.

4. Freeze for 10 minutes before serving.

Strawberry Icebox Casserole

Yield: Serves 10 | Prep Time: 15 minutes | Refrigerate: 4 hours

Starting with fresh berries and basil, this dessert is unique and fresh for a hot summer day, and it's one of my favorites to demonstrate at live cooking events. Eat with a spoon or use your hands to pull apart the shortbread pieces. It's perfect for any brunch or daytime dessert-eating occasion.

INGREDIENTS

3½ cups heavy cream

2 (8-ounce) containers mascarpone cream, room temperature

½ cup plus 2 tablespoons powdered sugar

2 teaspoons vanilla extract

¼ teaspoon kosher salt

90 shortbread cookies

2 (16-ounce) packages strawberries, hulled and sliced, plus extra strawberries for serving

1 banana, sliced

Fresh basil, for garnish

DIRECTIONS

1. In the bowl of a stand mixer, whip the cream, mascarpone, powdered sugar, vanilla, and salt together until the mixture forms medium-stiff peaks.

2. Spread a thin layer of the cream mixture in a 9 × 13-inch baking dish and cover with a layer of shortbread cookies. Spread one-quarter of the remaining cream mixture over the cookies and top with one-third of the strawberries. Cover the strawberries with another layer of cookies, then spread with one-quarter of the cream and one-third of the strawberries. Repeat with the remaining shortbread, one-quarter of the cream, and the remaining strawberries. Spread the remaining cream on top.

3. Cover with plastic wrap and refrigerate for 4 hours. Serve with extra strawberries and fresh basil leaves.

Hidden S'mores Casserole

Yield: Serves 8 to 10 | Prep Time: 20 minutes | Cook Time: 15 minutes

My s'mores never looked like this by the bonfire! But no bonfire is needed to make this layered s'more dessert. I absolutely love the flaky "burnt" crust that covers the marshmallows, chocolate, and graham cracker crumbs. If you have a blowtorch, char the top, and the hint of smoky flavor will remind you of the campfire version of this fun dessert.

INGREDIENTS

2 sheets puff pastry

1 pound cream cheese, room temperature

1 cup sugar

7 ounces marshmallow crème

9 graham crackers

8 tablespoons unsalted butter, melted

1 cup semisweet chocolate chips

1 cup bittersweet chocolate chips

2 cups mini marshmallows

DIRECTIONS

1. Preheat the oven to 375°F and lightly coat a 9 × 13-inch baking dish with cooking spray.

2. Roll out 1 sheet of puff pastry, place it in the baking dish, and prick the dough several times with a fork.

3. In a medium bowl, combine the cream cheese and ¾ cup of the sugar. Add the marshmallow crème and mix well. Spread the mixture evenly on top of the puff pastry.

4. Crush the graham crackers into fine crumbs, add 2 tablespoons of the sugar and 3 tablespoons of the melted butter, and mix together. Layer the graham cracker mixture over the marshmallow crème mixture. Sprinkle the chocolate chips over the graham cracker crumbs, then sprinkle the marshmallows on top.

5. Prick the second sheet of puff pastry with a fork and then place it on the marshmallows.

6. Brush the remaining melted butter over the dough and sprinkle with the remaining sugar.

7. Bake for 12 to 15 minutes, until golden brown and the top is puffed. Toast the crust with a blowtorch, if desired. Serve.

NOTES

To toast your crust (optional), you will need a blowtorch. You can find one at any hardware store, or order online.

Favorite Apple Fritter Casserole

Yield: Serves 6 to 8 | Prep Time: 20 minutes | Cook Time: 30 minutes

Hidden beneath the pile of Granny Smith and Fuji apples in this casserole lies a layer of flaky golden croissants. Cooked in a thick orange syrup and tossed together, the apples are coated with cinnamon and baked until your entire home smells of fall.

INGREDIENTS

6 tablespoons unsalted butter

½ cup light brown sugar

½ cup granulated sugar

3 Granny Smith apples, diced

4 Fuji apples, 3 diced and 1 sliced for garnish

½ cup plus 1 tablespoon apple butter

1 teaspoon cornstarch

6 large croissants, cut into chunks

½ cup heavy cream

3 large eggs, lightly beaten

1 teaspoon vanilla extract

¼ teaspoon apple pie spice

½ cup powdered sugar

DIRECTIONS

1. Preheat the oven to 375°F and lightly coat a 9 × 13-inch baking dish with cooking spray.

2. In a large skillet, melt the butter over medium heat. Add both sugars and stir until combined.

3. Add the apples, reserving the sliced apple for garnish, and simmer, stirring, for 5 minutes or until the apples begin to soften.

4. Stir in 1 tablespoon of the apple butter and the cornstarch and remove from the heat.

5. Spread the croissant pieces in the bottom of the baking dish and top with the apple mixture.

6. Combine the cream, eggs, vanilla, apple pie spice, and remaining apple butter and pour over the apples.

7. Bake for 25 minutes. Top with the powdered sugar, garnish with apple slices, and serve.

Easy Peach and Plum Casserole Cake

Yield: Serves 6 to 8 | Prep Time: 5 minutes | Cook Time: 45 minutes

If you have ever made a one-pan peach cake, this is similar—but in a casserole dish and baked until caramelized. Topped with plums and sugar, its crispy coating contrasts perfectly with the gooey center. Serve hot with vanilla ice cream, and you will probably be eating it right out of the dish.

INGREDIENTS

2 (16-ounce) cans peaches in heavy syrup

1 (15.25-ounce) box yellow cake mix

8 tablespoons cold unsalted butter

¼ cup light brown sugar

½ teaspoon ground cinnamon

2 plums, pitted and sliced

Vanilla ice cream, for serving

DIRECTIONS

1. Preheat the oven to 375°F and lightly coat a 9-inch round cake pan with cooking spray.

2. Pour the peaches with their juices into the baking dish and cover with the dry cake mix; press down to combine slightly. Cut the butter into thin slices and arrange on top of the cake mix. Sprinkle the brown sugar and cinnamon on top. Bake for 45 minutes until bubbling and golden. Garnish with the sliced plums and serve with vanilla ice cream.

Pear and Cranberry Cobbler

Yield: Serves 6–8 | Prep Time: 30 minutes | Cook Time: 1 hour | Refrigerate: 20 minutes

In this cobbler, the subtle sweetness of the pears perfectly complements the tart bursts of the cranberries. And everything is better with whipped topping.

INGREDIENTS

Cobbler Dough

2 cups all-purpose flour

6 tablespoons plus 1 teaspoon sugar

2 teaspoons baking powder

¼ teaspoon kosher salt

6 tablespoons unsalted butter, cold, cut into ¼-inch cubes

½ cup plus 1 tablespoon heavy cream

1 large egg yolk

Filling

3 pounds Bosc or Bartlett pears, cored and cut into ½-inch wedges

2 cups fresh or frozen cranberries

½ cup granulated sugar

¼ cup light brown sugar

1 tablespoon orange juice plus 2 teaspoons grated zest

½ teaspoon ground cinnamon

¼ teaspoon ground cardamom

Vanilla Mascarpone Whipped Topping

1 cup mascarpone cheese, room temperature

1 cup heavy cream

½ teaspoon vanilla bean paste

¼ cup sugar

DIRECTIONS

1. Preheat the oven to 425°F and butter a 9-inch deep-dish pie plate.

2. For the cobbler dough: Whisk together the flour, 6 tablespoons of the sugar, the baking powder, and salt. Scatter the butter cubes over the flour mixture and cut in with a pastry cutter until the dough looks like coarse cornmeal. Stir together ½ cup of the cream and the egg yolk. Add to the flour mixture and toss with a fork until the ingredients come together.

3. Turn the dough out onto a lightly floured surface and knead gently together. Wrap and let rest in the refrigerator for 20 minutes.

4. For the filling: While the dough rests, combine all the filling ingredients and pour into the baking dish.

5. Pat the dough out, tear or cut into 3-inch pieces, and place them on the filling. Brush the dough with the remaining 1 tablespoon cream and sprinkle with the remaining 1 teaspoon sugar. Bake for 45 to 55 minutes, until bubbling and golden. Let cool slightly.

6. For the vanilla mascarpone whipped topping: Whip together the mascarpone, cream, and vanilla until combined. Add the sugar slowly and beat until fluffy and you have soft peaks. Serve on top of the warm cobbler.

Acknowledgments

I want to thank everyone. To write a big long list with all of your names. Because it's hard to believe that I have gotten to where I am, and I know that I wouldn't have if it weren't for you.

You know who you are if you're reading this. You, among many, have inspired, helped, and cared for me along the way, getting me to this moment where I am writing these very words. As I continue to cook, to style food, to photograph, and to write, I will slowly but surely thank you all individually, because for all that you have done, and much more, I am so incredibly grateful.

With that said, I want to begin giving thanks with this first book by acknowledging my childhood. I grew up in Minnesota, where we made forts at our cabin in the woods, climbed trees in the summer, and flooded the backyard with water to skate on in the frigid winter months. We shucked the corn we ate, said please and thank you, and when eating in the farmhouse, we joined the clean-plate club without fail. I am thankful for those who raised me this way: my grandparents, my parents, my aunts and uncles, my cousins and my brother. Thank you to those who instilled in me what it means to be "Minnesota nice" and for teaching me that a Midwestern upbringing is special.

Thank you to my incredible culinary and creative team at Prime Publishing: Tom Krawczyk, my photographer and videographer and Chris Hammond, Judith Hines, and Marlene Stolfo, my culinary test kitchen geniuses. To word masters and editors Bryn Clark and Jessica Thelander. And to my amazing editor and friend, Kara Rota. This book was a team effort, filled with collaboration and creativity that reached no limits.

Index

About the Author

After receiving her masters in culinary arts at Auguste Escoffier in Avignon, France, Addie stayed in France to learn from Christian Etienne at his three-Michelin-star restaurant. Upon leaving France, she spent the next several years working with restaurant groups. She worked in the kitchen for Daniel Boulud and moved coast to coast with Thomas Keller building a career in management, restaurant openings, and brand development. She later joined Martha Stewart Living Omnimedia, where she worked with the editorial team as well as in marketing and sales. While living in New York, Addie completed her bachelor's degree in organizational behavior. Upon leaving New York, Addie joined gravitytank, an innovation consultancy in Chicago. As a culinary designer at gravitytank, Addie designed new food products for companies large and small. She created edible prototypes for clients and research participants to taste and experience, some of which you may see in stores today. In 2015, she debuted on the Food Network, where she competed on *Cutthroat Kitchen*, and won!

Addie is the executive producer for RecipeLion. Addie oversees and creates culinary content for multiple Web platforms and communities, leads video strategy, and oversees the production of in-print books. Addie is passionate about taking easy recipes and making them elegant, without making them complicated. From fine dining to entertaining, to innovation and test kitchens, Addie's experience with food makes these recipes unique and delicious.

Addie and her husband, Alex, live in Lake Forest, Illinois, with their happy puppy, Paisley. Addie is actively involved with youth culinary programs in the Chicagoland area, serving on the board of a bakery and catering company that employs at-risk youth. She is a healthy-food teacher for first-graders in a low-income school district and, aside from eating and entertaining with friends and family, she loves encouraging kids to be creative in the kitchen!